Singing from the Soul

Frontispiece: Curtain call, *Carmen,* Vienna, January 1990.

JOSÉ CARRERAS
Singing from the Soul

An Autobiography

NEC IGNI
CEDIT
NEC
FERRO

Y·C·P·PUBLICATIONS, INC.

SEATTLE

Translation Staff
  German language specialists: Barbara von Schalburg Ramos, Dr. Adela Gebr
  Translation editors: JOHN ELLIS THOMAS, MARIA L. VALDEMI, with S.L. Yu
Edited by WALTER PRICE
Consultant for Discography, Videography, and picture legends: Fritz Krammer,
secretary to José Carreras

Project editor and book designer: Sun L. Yu
See production acknowledgements in the back of the book.

Publisher's cataloging in publication data
  Carreras, José. Singing From The Soul. An autobiography.
   Translation of *Singen Mit Der Seele.*
   Library of Courage Series - One.

   Includes index.
   Discography: p.
   Videography: p.
  1. Carreras, José. 2. Singers - Biography. I. Title.

ISBN 1-878756-89-3

Library of Congress Catalogue Card Number: 90-71130

10 9 8 7 6 5 4 3 2 1

Printed and bound in Singapore

This book may be ordered from the
publisher, see order form in the
back. But try your bookstore first.

LIBRARY OF COURAGE - 1

To Alberto and Julia

Contents

Contents

I wish to thank Herbert Hufnagl, my Viennese friend,
for the realization of this book.

José Carreras

Singing from the Soul

1

My Wish Comes True

July 21, 1988.

A magnificent day—*my* day. Tonight I sing again in my beloved Barcelona. I am alive! Worry, fear and pain—those gloomy bedfellows—have left me. The nightmare is over. My last few weeks have been peaceful, filled with joy and hope.

My battle against leukemia started only a year ago, but those long, cruel months of treatment seem light years away. I have survived the most ruthless time of my life—and here I am. Better yet, I can sing. I am whole, again. It's really my day—the happiest of my life! I want to sing better than ever before. I want to say to the opera world, to everyone who knows, loves, and lives opera, "Look! I'm back! I'm with you again!"

It's almost impossible for me to describe the thrill of feeling so alive. I want to shout with joy and have the winds carry my message to the ends of the earth. I want to give thanks for science and the doctors. I want to thank my family. And I want to thank God. While I was undergoing treatment I had endless time to meditate. Each day His true power became more apparent to me, and, finally, I discovered I believe very deeply. It's obvious to me now that fear is a poor reason for faith in Him. We shouldn't wait for a lightning bolt to bring us to our knees . . . .

Tonight's concert is a wish come true: I can't imagine a better way to thank the people who helped me so much. I want to sing for them, to let my voice show the gratitude in my heart. Though the occasion is also to benefit the clinic where I was first admitted, and to celebrate the centennial of Barcelona's Universal Exposition, the most exciting thing for me tonight—and what I want most—is to be able to embrace the audience with my voice, to say to each person, "I am grateful for your tremendous support and affection over these past months; it was a great comfort. Let me sing for you, for each one of you. It's my way of saying 'Thank you.'"

I've been thinking about this evening, trying to imagine what it'll be like. How will I feel when I walk out under Barcelona's Arch of Triumph? A few days ago, a close friend told me, laughingly, to take a strong tranquilizer before the performance. I said, "Great! But when everyone has gone, I hope you'll kindly remember to come to my dressing room and wake me up." It was a little joke then, but today I'm really worried what might happen if I go on stage so emotionally charged. No, I'm not ashamed to show my feelings. But if I become too emotional, I won't be able to sing, and the whole event will be ruined. What a disaster, to stand there blubbering, "A thousand thanks for coming tonight. You touch me so deeply, I'm going to cry. Sorry, I'm too choked up to make a sound, so I had better leave now." No, I can't let this happen. Carreras the artist must prevail over Carreras the man!

But at the moment, all this worry about breaking down is academic, nothing more than conjecture. I can't anticipate how difficult it will be to keep my professionalism at this performance which is still two hours away. I must put this aside and face it when the time comes. I have enough to think about. My God! I am terrified at the thought of appearing on the stage again.

When I first fell ill, survival was my only goal. But it's human nature never to be satisfied. True, I was overjoyed when, toward the end of May, 1988, the blood transfusions stopped, the medications were halted, and I was finally allowed to go home. What a relief to hear the doctors say, "José, you've made it; you're well. You can do anything you want." I was cured!

But nagging doubts marred my happiness: could I sing? What would it mean to me, to live but not to sing? I had to find out. Science gave me back my health, but what did it do to my voice? I knew very clearly I would never be one hundred percent myself if I couldn't sing. I'd be missing something in my life so much that I'd find it an immeasurable loss.

On the other hand, I knew that I could live up to any necessity; I would somehow survive this tragedy and remain functional. I've always believed that in each of us there are hidden resources waiting to be discovered. A turn of fate that forces us to look within ourselves can be a gift. If I could no longer sing, I'd find a fresh, new reason for living. Of course, nothing could be as rewarding to me as singing, but I'd find something else to do, something that would make me happy and give meaning to my life.

Still, that agonizing question was always on my mind. My voice, was it still there? I knew that leukemia treatments could affect one's vocal cords; I was tortured with anxiety. In March 1988, long before the doctors gave me the green light, I decided to conduct a small test in the shower. Locking myself in the bathroom, I ran through several simple vocal exercises. Not too bad . . . . Then I tried a few fragments from Puccini's *Manon Lescaut*. I sang along with a tape I had recorded in May 1987 with Kiri Te Kanawa under the direction of Riccardo Chailly. The tape had been mailed to me by the record company just that week. Singing along with a recording was always my favourite way to rehearse. When I was a student I played my great idols; now I use my own recordings. It's a wonderful challenge, pitting myself against myself. And this comparison relieved much of my present anxiety.

I didn't sound so bad after all! In fact, I was rather pleased with myself. This impromptu singing-in-the-shower experiment raised my hopes and boosted my morale. However, Dr. Cyril Rozman, Chief of Hematology at the Hospital Clinico in Barcelona, didn't share my enthusiasm. When he found out what I had done, he warned me to be more cautious, saying the doctors would let me know when it was safe to resume vocalizing. When I finally received their medical blessing, all sorts of restrictions were attached: I was to be careful, begin slowly, and not overdo it.

I was anxious for my scheduled visit with Dr. Heinz Kursten, an internationally eminent doctor of laryngology in Vienna. A visit to his office is an almost obligatory stop off for opera singers from all over the world. I had known Dr. Kursten for years and trusted his judgement completely. When I was undergoing treatment in Seattle, he had phoned me several times. We'd both been afraid, all along, that the chemotherapy and radiation would damage my vocal cords, so when Dr. Kursten saw me he was most surprised that I had come through it all in such good shape. Still, he advised me to go slowly, prescribing short vocal exercises—a half-hour in the morning and another half-hour in the afternoon. I followed his advice. Accompanying myself on the piano, I began to work on a programme that would be right for my first comeback appearances.

My pianist, Vincenzo Scalera, arrived in Barcelona a few days ago. We've been rehearsing every day, but always with restraint, not too long, not too hard. I feel ready for tonight's performance. I'm truly content, and I'm as nervous as always before a concert or a performance. We opera singers realize that we're at the mercy of nature, so dependent on a few centimeters of delicate tissue. In the end, it doesn't matter how musical or talented we are, how well we know the score, or how long we've rehearsed. We can't do a thing if our vocal cords stretch, become irritated, or get infected. Our careers hang on these two incredibly thin tissues. No wonder our anxiety about them follows us around the world. We each have our own morning ritual, a unique way to intuitively sense or actually test this mechanism to see if it's still working.

This morning, mine works. Relieved, I venture out onto the balcony of our house in l'Ametlla del Valles. In the garden below, I see my children, Julia and Alberto, romping with our two dogs, Vasco, a German shepherd, and Higgins, a setter. (The children took the name "Higgins" from the television show, *Magnum P.I.* But I'll say more about that later.)

My children! They've been such a wonderful discovery to me. If you could only understand what a hectic life an opera star leads. We're always in demand—always somewhere else, never at home. I'm just beginning to understand what it means to be a father. I'm just getting to know my children. This is the first time I've had the chance to observe them in their own surroundings. Dressing rooms, airports, restaurants—these are places where you meet people, not places where you get to know them. And yet, for so many years, such moments and places were all we had. Yes, my conscience bothered me. I knew that Alberto and

Julia were really wonderful children—but I knew so little about them. I didn't know anything about their everyday joys or sorrows; I saw only a fraction of their personalities. Now, I'm busy catching up.

I can hardly believe it: Alberto is already fifteen. No longer a boy, he's beginning to think and act like a man. I can talk to him about almost anything. But what I love most about him is his marvelous sense of humour. I genuinely enjoy people who can inspire honest laughter. What a wonderfully simple delight it is to be able to laugh with my own son.

As for my daughter Julia, I've always loved her helplessly. But the past few months have convinced me that she is by far the sweetest and the most affectionate child in the world. I couldn't refuse her anything. I'm completely in her power.

The children suffered a lot while I was ill, although my wife tried to protect them from the stress as much as she could. Mercedes is an exceptional mother who always knows exactly what to reveal. She told Alberto and Julia about my illness and even explained how serious the situation was. But she never dramatized it. She refused to let sentimentality and gloom invade their childhood. Every question and every situation was handled in a way that let the children believe everything would turn out all right. Still, it was difficult for them because they were constantly harassed at school with the same heartbreaking questions. How's your father? Where is he now? Is he coming back?

My relationship with my children is growing deeper and stronger now that I'm home. The day I was well enough to play a little tennis with Alberto, he was as happy as if he had received a present. Alberto put me on a high pedestal. I'm surprised how much he tries to imitate me. Of course, what father doesn't wish for, and enjoy, such admiration?

All of this makes me happy, but at the same time it hurts. I think of how much I have missed in my private life, being on tour for so many years.

Yesterday, the 20th of July, was Julia's tenth birthday. One of her presents was a camera, and I was delighted to be her model while she played "photographer." During the rehearsal for tonight's concert, she snapped pictures of me from every possible angle! I had wanted to hold my comeback recital right on Julia's birthday, but for reasons beyond my control, that schedule couldn't be arranged. Regardless, I still consider my performance tonight to be for Julia, a slightly belated birthday present.

It's early yet, so I spend time walking through the garden, something I've done many times during the past few weeks. I find myself stopping and standing in awe before such simple, ordinary things—things I never noticed or used to consider trivial and insignificant. Now I enjoy watching the birds; I'm amazed by the colours in a butterfly's wings and the lush vegetation that surrounds me. I marvel at the splendid cacti that border this side of the house. I submerge myself in the sounds that are all around me. It's as if my senses have been fine-tuned. Everything I see, hear, or touch is intensely magnified. It is said that as we age we open our eyes to beauty and become more receptive to the marvels and secrets of nature. If this is true, then in just these past few months, I've become a very, very old man.

Several days ago, I had a beautiful dream: I was stretched out on the deck of a large ship that was sailing in the open sea. I was watching the sunrise, the rapid bursting and blending of gorgeous colours. My brother, Alberto, was there, telling me a story. As so often happens with dreams, I can't quite remember what the story was about, but I do remember that it was very funny. In fact, I laughed so hard tears came to my eyes, at which point, I woke up. Later that day, while we were having dinner, I discovered that one of our dinner guests had a reputation for interpreting dreams, so I told him about mine. He said that it was a good omen to dream about a ship, and that if the ship were heading toward a new shore—that was even better. At this point he quoted from the Chinese Book of Wisdom, *I Ching,* "It is good to cross the great waters." When the dream-scene occurs at dawn, be said, it's an even better sign, and the dreamer should expect a "productive morning." Although I couldn't vouch for our guest's explanation of my dream, his interpretation fascinated me. Ever since that day, I have felt that this dream was given to me as a sign, a foretelling of my new life.

It's time to leave for tonight's concert, which I have started to consider as my "second debut." There's no doubt in my mind that this debut is much more important to me than my first. I'm sure I will find it to be much more emotional.

I drive the twenty-five miles to Barcelona. It's such a joy to be behind the wheel again! I have a passion for driving, and I confess that over the years I've indulged myself. It's such a pity that all the years I was busy, or ill and confined, my cars just sat in the garage.

I usually arrive for a performance well ahead of time, but today that may be a problem. The streets near the concert area have been cordoned off by the police. I can barely move forward; there are so many people milling around. Someone recognizes me and points to a banner hung across a building: "Josep, we are happy to have you back!" A stagehand tells me that hundreds of these people started appearing very early in the afternoon just to get good places in the standing room areas. The day is unbearably hot, but this early crowd is coping fairly well with the heat. They have brought along drinks, food, and umbrellas.

Yesterday evening we held a rehearsal here at the Arch. When I sang a few bars to test the installation of the audio system, there was applause. How in the world do fans find out about these unscheduled events? Rumours spread fast.

The area around the Arch of Triumph is crammed with people, but I can still move about easily. The Arch is a gigantic, impressive structure, built in 1888 as the main entrance to the Universal Exposition. The organizers of tonight's concert, the Citizen Commission for the Commemoration of the Centennial of the Universal Exposition, were worried about crowd control, so they have installed a line of fencing across the front of the Arch. A stage, constructed under the Arch, extends across the entire width of the monument. It is about six feet high, enough for those far away to get a good view. And the immense stage is so huge that the grand piano appears to be just a speck. Microphone towers have been installed on both sides of the stage, as well as along the Lluis Companys Boulevard; four gigantic Eidefor screens have been set up in the nearby park. With all the paraphernalia, even people who are two streets away from the Arch can see and hear what's happening on stage.

Thousands of seats, reserved for ticketholders, have been placed in front of the stage. This is a benefit concert, so each ticket is a contribution to the Foundation for the Fight Against Leukemia, an organization I created and will say more about later. Patrons donated 250,000 pesetas each to sit in the first row of chairs, the "zero row." A small barrier separates the seating sections from the standing room areas in the rest of the park. There's plenty of standing room, and it's all free.

In two hours, the recital will begin. We estimated the

concert would draw an audience of 30,000, but the police warn us that, even though it's still early, there are more people than expected. In fact, more than we dreamed possible. The Lluis Companys Boulevard is jammed, yet people keep streaming in.

With all of this unexpected commotion, excitement is running rife. Many of my friends and acquaintances manage to find their way to the makeshift dressing room to wish me well. I appreciate their words of encouragement as well as the deference and respect they show me. Suddenly, my colleague and friend, Giacomo Aragall, arrives; then Agnes Baltsa; and of course, Montserrat Caballé. Although Montserrat had a long-standing contract for engagements in Madrid, she has asked to be excused to attend my concert. Above all else, she wanted to be here for my comeback celebration, to be with me for my second debut.

2

"I'm Sorry, You Have Leukemia"

I SERIOUSLY debated whether or not to talk about my illness in this book. I know an opera singer is a public figure, and part of being famous and in the "public eye" means we sacrifice our rights to completely private lives. But just how far into our private lives does the public have a right to see? I don't mean to exaggerate or complain about this. But we face the problem continually in one way or another. What *are* the limits? When an opera singer is indisposed and performances are cancelled, that's news. When the illness is long and the explanations few, the public gets curious. The question of "invasion of privacy" is a thorny one.

I've been asked why in the beginning both my doctors and my family braced themselves against revealing my true illness. Their brief, official statement to the press was that I had "an acute change in blood composition." To give that vague diagnosis had been my idea. I didn't want pity from anyone, least of all my close friends or fans. I must confess that at the time I thought everything would be simple: "José Carreras, the tenor, is ill. He'll be better soon and sing again. In the meantime, life goes on. That's all."

Unfortunately, it was naive of me to think the public would be satisfied with such ambiguous explanations. Many newsmen, especially tabloid reporters, started asking questions and when they couldn't get answers, they made up their own. As a result they circulated the wildest and often insulting rumours, which hurt me a great deal. Their curiosity was insatiable. One group managed to discover what kind of medicines and the type of treatment I was receiving at the Hospital Clinico in Barcelona. Armed with these clues, they consulted a hematologist in Madrid and lost no time publishing his long-distance diagnosis.

I was not the only one hurt by the media insensitivity. I know for a fact that there were patients at the Hospital who didn't know they had leukemia. Doctors, for whatever reason, may think it best to keep such dire news from their patients—and sometimes from their families as well. Imagine how shocked you'd be if you were casually watching the news on television and heard the newscaster list the medications that you—or your cousin, or your wife, or your friend—are taking. Suddenly you realize that whatever terrible thing is happening to José Carreras is also happening to you or to someone you love.

In all of this persistent muckraking, the photographers took first prize. Several climbed trees in the hospital yard, hoping to get a glimpse of me as I passed in front of a window. Three of the more daring were caught when they tried to slip into my hospital room disguised as doctors—hiding their cameras and their intentions under those pure white hospital gowns. In fact, one of them confessed that a magazine had offered "two million pesetas for one picture of Carreras in bed."

Another group of these bloodhounds caught the scent

when it was rumoured I was being moved to another clinic for gum surgery. Waiting in ambush at the clinic door, they successfully got away with a snapshot of me wearing a surgical half-mask. The picture was published in many newspapers and magazines, sometimes with the silliest captions. To set the record straight, my mouth was covered because my cheek was swollen. But enough of this.

Let's return to my concern over whether I should include anything about my illness in this book and why I decided I would. During those frightfully long months I spent in one hospital or another, something wonderful happened. I received thousands of letters. The surprising thing, almost unbelievable to me, was that many of these letters were from people who had nothing to do with opera. They were from people who read about me in the newspaper or who just heard what happened and wanted to encourage me. Some sent me small presents, a poem they'd written, or a personally hand-made gift.

I suddenly realized these people were not taking their time to write me because I was famous or because I was an opera singer. It wasn't that at all. This wasn't applause; this wasn't fan mail. This was pure kindness, empathy, the love of one human being for another. What a wonderful, new experience this was. It made me want to fight my way back all the harder, especially during the worst moments of my illness.

Later, I came to the conclusion that since I found such comfort and strength in knowing that even strangers cared, I should do the same for others who are suffering as I suffered. I care about them—and I want them to know. It was then I decided to write openly about what happened to me while I was ill. I decided to reveal everything, from beginning to end . . . . Even if only one person draws courage and confidence from my words, then my decision to talk about this most intimate and private part of my life will be rewarded.

My problems started to surface early in the summer of 1987. I was feeling exhausted and depressed, but blamed my fatigue on the stress of a full schedule. In April, I appeared as Canio in *Pagliacci*. (I didn't know it at the time, but the 29th of April 1987, at La Scala in Milan, would be my last opera appearance for a long, long time.) May, too, was a busy month. I had to cancel several stage engagements because of a leg injury. I spent this borrowed time in the recording studio. In June, there was less to do, so I went to Vienna and worked on this book. The diversion was nice. It felt good to be doing something completely different.

Anticipating a rather light summer schedule, I hoped to rest and recuperate during July and August. Only a few opera performances were scheduled for the summer, one of them *Carmen,* with Agnes Baltsa, in Ravenna. I was also looking forward to filming *La Bohème* under the direction of Luigi Comencini, a commitment that could extend into September. Filming is hard work, but in a different way than performing on stage. There are long periods of nothing to do but sit and wait, and I hoped this would be an ideal time to continue working on my book. Suddenly, everything went wrong!

On July 5, I gave a concert in San Sebastian. This was my last stage appearance for more than a year. That night I flew in a private jet to Paris—the only way I could make it on time to start filming *La Bohème* at six the next morning. On the set, things quickly fell into place, and everything ran like clockwork for the first few days. Then a tooth, implanted a few months earlier, started to bother me. I went to have it checked, and the dentist thought I might have a gum infection. He prescribed antibiotics. I took the medication, but didn't get any better; soon I felt worse.

I couldn't think about filming in my condition. On Monday, July 13, I apologized to Director Comencini, and with the help of a friend who had contacts in Paris I checked into the American Hospital there. Something was wrong. I knew I had to find out exactly what was the matter with me.

I had blood tests done, an electrocardiogram, and several other exploratory tests that comprised a complete physical check-up. I left the hospital that evening, knowing the results wouldn't be ready until the following day. When I returned, the doctor who had examined me the day before was noncommittal. He advised me to check into the hospital for more tests. He said my blood count was low, but this could be a reaction to all the antibiotics I was taking for the tooth infection. He hedged on the details. It was only later that I found out my pre-admission test showed a dangerously low level of blood platelets: ninety percent lower than that of a healthy person.

The next day, with Paris in a festive mood and all of France celebrating Bastille Day, I had to face the awful, harsh reality. That morning Professor Jean Bernard, one of the foremost hematologists in the world, came to see me. I thought to myself, "When a famous specialist shows up in your hospital room at ten o'clock in the morning on a national holiday, there must be a good reason. Something must be really wrong."

Professor Bernard told me that more tests, including a spinal tap, or lumbar puncture, would be needed to confirm a diagnosis. *A spinal tap.* The words hit home. With a flood of emotion, I remembered what had happened in Barcelona more than twenty years ago. The doctors performed a spinal tap on my mother and found cancer in its last stages. Considering my family history and what I knew about the disease, I began to suspect leukemia. I finally asked one doctor, point-blank, if this was my case. When he said the possibility couldn't be ruled out, it was as good as telling me I was right. Otherwise, he would have simply said "No" and put an end to my anxiety.

My brother, Alberto, flew to Paris to be with me as soon as he heard I'd been admitted to the hospital. He was at my side when, on July 16, Professor Bernard came into my room to announce, "The results are in. I'm sorry to be the one to tell you, but *you have leukemia.*"

It was strange. I knew exactly what Professor Bernard was going to say. But when I actually heard the words, they went off in my head like a time bomb.

Hope is something we hold onto until the very last moment. And once it goes away, how quickly we try to bring it back! Even while Professor Bernard's horrifying words hung in the air, a new confidence was filling my heart: "Perhaps I *can* overcome this." And I became more hopeful as I focused on Professor Bernard's professional and reassuring words. "Don't worry too much. Nowadays, it isn't so terrible to have leukemia. We have new drugs, new treatments. Fight, and you'll win."

Alberto stood quietly by my side. I knew he was wishing he could change places with me, that he'd rather be the one in bed, facing whatever was in store for me. I knew exactly how he felt because I'd have wished the same if our positions were reversed. This is the kind of loyalty that marks our family. Our parents brought us up to believe that the lives of our brothers and sisters are as important as our own. My wife, my sister-in-law, and my brother-in-law also think this way. In the difficult months that followed, our family's sense of solidarity and belonging was tested to its extreme.

The idea of leukemia was frightening to my family because, three years earlier, my sister-in-law Marisa's cousin had died of it. She was someone exactly my age; I remember going to school with her for a while. When her leukemia was discovered, she was a practicing doctor at the Hospital Clinico. And still all attempts to save her life failed.

My brother, Alberto, is nine years older, but there has always been a special bond between us. That night I couldn't sleep. And I was grateful that Alberto stayed up with me. This was probably the worst night of our lives, but I treasure it because it brought us even closer together. We confided in each other, talking about things that we both knew but had never felt the need to express before. We also discussed the future and tried to anticipate all that might happen. Alberto promised to tell me everything the doctors had to say. Everything, no more, no less. I didn't want lies to protect me. I felt I had to know exactly what was going on. How else could I put up a good fight? From the very beginning, I felt sure that I would be strong enough to endure—and lucky enough to win.

We also discussed another serious issue. I told Alberto that I was willing to submit to any kind of treatment, no matter how torturous, but I drew the line at being a guinea pig. I wanted no experimentation, period. And, if the treatments failed, I didn't want doctors to keep me artificially alive with fancy machines and equipment. The thought of lying there, mechanically wired, to look alive but not to be alive, filled me with terror. Alberto promised to respect my wishes.

I had to set those things straight with Alberto. His promises were insurance, just in case something happened. But from the beginning, I trusted in science and had a strong feeling that the doctors were right, that I would be cured. That night I made up my mind, not just to take up the fight, but to put all of this behind me as quickly as possible. I was full of hope and ready to play the hand I'd been dealt. If, out of a hundred leukemia patients, the odds were that one would survive, then I was going to be that one. I didn't just say this to myself, I *believed* it.

3

The Path
of Thorns Begins

On Saturday, July 18, 1987, I flew home
from Paris in a special Austrian ambulance jet that had
been brought in from Innsbruck. Alberto was with me; he
hadn't left my side for the past few days. We had both considered my staying in Paris for treatment, but after discussing all the pros and cons with my doctor and friend, Jordi
Permanyer, we decided that Barcelona would be our best
bet. Doctor Cyril Rozman, one of the foremost hematologists in the world, was on the staff of the Hospital Clinico.
We also thought if I were to be hospitalized or in treatment
for very long, it would be much easier for my family to visit
and help if I were closer to home.

My chemotherapy began that next Monday.

And so did the complications. The disease already had
such a hold on me that my immune system barely func-
tioned. Right at the outset, what the doctors feared most
happened: I developed pneumonia. My life was in serious
danger, and only heavy doses of medication helped to
bring down the fever and fight off the infection. I pulled
out of that crisis, but for a long time afterward my situation

remained critical. Even the slightest virus or infection was life-threatening, so I was confined to a germ-free room and no one, absolutely no one, was allowed to visit me. I understood that these restrictions were necessary, but I felt physically separated from everyone and everything I knew and loved—a feeling of being shut off from my real world.

Acute lymphoblastic leukemia, a frightening diagnosis. If it's not treated, it can kill you within a few months, and in the worst cases, a few days. It starts in the bone marrow where the blood forms, and with every drop of new blood death comes closer. This is the evil of leukemia: the cancer lives and grows in the blood, a flowing medium. This insidious disease travels easily through the bloodstream, and neither the radiologists nor the surgeons can stop it. They try to arrest it with chemotherapy, which means they inject poisons into the bloodstream to kill the cancerous cells, but very few people are completely cured by this treatment. A long-term improvement, a *remission*, is the most they can hope for.

There is one other way to fight the enemy and have a better chance for survival. If the cancerous cells can't be completely stopped or changed while in the bloodstream, there is the chance they can be destroyed at the source—within the bone marrow itself. A bone marrow transplant offers the greatest hope for a permanent cure. This is the treatment of choice, but the treatment itself is a path of thorns.

When I think how close I came to dying this past year, I find it strange that I was never afraid. I accepted my fate. I had leukemia, and there wasn't a thing I could do about it. But I didn't surrender. I would hold onto hope. Like every other patient, I had my ups and downs, feeling good one day, miserable the next. But through it all, I believed that I was going to make it. There were times when I thought, "I

can't take it anymore!" But I never said "Stop! I don't want
to go on . . . ."

At the start of my treatments, I remembered what
Friedrich Nietzsche, the German philosopher I so admire,
once wrote. According to this wise man, it's important to
"calm the imagination of the patient so that at least he does
not suffer more from his thoughts about the illness than
from the illness itself. I kept these words in mind and
worked hard to control my thoughts. I refused to let my
fears take over. I knew I couldn't waste time feeling sorry
for myself; what good would it do to keep blaming fate for
such a raw deal? The victim who bemoans his lot is already
half lost.

Nevertheless, I couldn't help wondering, "Why me?"
Was it the luck of the draw, like the lottery, a one-in-a-mil-
lion chance? Was it because life had been too good to me,
and now I had to pay the price? Or was I being punished for
something I had done? No, it couldn't be that. I looked
around and saw other leukemia patients—three-year-old
children—or even babies just a few months old. They were
totally innocent. They had no debts to pay. To be truthful, it
was when I compared myself to these tiny patients that I
realized how lucky I was. After all, I had had my chance to
live at least half a lifetime. And I had been healthy for so
many years. What were their chances for saying that?

During this time, it helped me to think about how much
I had to lose if I were to die. My children. My family. All the
people I love. My profession, my music. For these things,
I'd fight like a lion. *"I must hold on to all this,"* I told myself. I
hammered this thought into my head every day, over and
over, and it strengthened my will to survive.

Nothing was easy at first. In fact, during the first few
days I spent in the Hospital Clinico, I couldn't concentrate
on anything. Books and magazines weren't any help and al-

though I had a TV set, a VCR, tape recorders, even my own tapes, I just couldn't get interested in any of them. The telephone was the exception. With a phone next to the bed, I lived up to my reputation as a dyed-in-the-wool phone conversationalist and talked to friends all over the world. Thank God, I couldn't receive incoming calls.

The phenomenal interest that the world outside the hospital showed in my case was unnerving. I wasn't expecting it, and it took me a while to get over the shock. I don't mean the interest of the reporters and photographers lying in wait outside the hospital. Alberto took care of them by hiring two security guards to block the door to my room. No. What caught me unaware and which I found intimidating at first, was the huge number of personal letters and telegrams that started piling up. People from all over the world were writing to me: the royal family of Spain, the political leaders of many countries, my friends and colleagues in the arts, theatre directors, and thousands of opera fans.

I was surprised and somewhat bewildered by it all, to be remembered by so many people. Marilyn Horne was giving a concert in Barcelona and sent a gigantic bouquet up to my room, an arrangement so big that all the nurses in the unit had flowers for a week. Grace Bumbry during a concert in Vienna dedicated a song to me. Gestures like this, no matter how big or small, ordinary or extraordinary, meant very much to me.

Neither can I forget all that my family went through; it was an awful period for them. As soon as I was admitted to the Hospital Clinico, they began an unending, tedious vigil. Day and night, someone from my family was always near, even when I was quarantined in a sterile room and we were limited to watching each other through a glass door and talking over a special telephone.

As I already mentioned, our family is close-knit, and we have always given each other a great deal of support, but this was the biggest problem we had ever had to face. And it lasted so long. The days dragged into weeks and then into months. I assured my family they could leave me alone for a while, that everything would be all right, but they wouldn't let up. Not for a day. I confess it made me very happy to have them stay close. Arranging to be near a loved one in the hospital for such a long time isn't easy. Now that I know what my family went through, I have a great deal of respect for the various international organizations established to help families keep up with this selfless task.

My first chemotherapy sessions took place from July 20 to August 10, a miserable three weeks. During chemotherapy, your body is pumped full of poison. You feel constantly, terribly nauseous. There's no end to the vomiting and diarrhea, so you're very weak. All the time the doctors keep puncturing you to take samples of your bone marrow for analyses. They must determine whether the chemotherapy is killing off the cancerous cells, giving you a chance for remission. If the cancer cells start to return after the first chemotherapy, things can get complicated. I was lucky. On August 12, a red-letter day for me, I passed the final, most important bone marrow test of the series. I was in remission.

Ten days later, I was transferred to the Quiron Clinic. I'd recovered enough from the chemotherapy to have an operation on my infected tooth, the problem that had seemed to lead into all this. But by now my medical history was complicated. Even a simple operation in my present condition was risky, so I was kept at the clinic for two days. But at last the wheel of fortune turned in my favour and I was released to spend a few days at home.

At this time I decided to learn everything I could about

leukemia and the different treatments the doctors were
planning for me. I wanted to know exactly what lay ahead.
Yet I must confess that once I found out, I was afraid to even
think about it. I tried to control the rising panic by telling
myself over and over again, "You must go through this hell,
there's no way out of it. If you want to be cured, this is the
price you must pay. Right now, it's horrible, but when it's
all over, everything will be wonderful."

But for a long time I felt light years away from anything
"wonderful." To add insult to injury, several newspapers
started publishing wild stories about my illness. Sometimes I think there are reporters who thrive on stealing lies
from each other. One story is published, another sees it
and dresses it up for his paper; his version is picked up by a
third who gives it his touch, and on and on. Many of these
so-called "news reports," actually wild guesses or outright
lies, appeared in Austria, West Germany, and especially in
Italy. Here I should mention that, on the whole, the press
was very fair to me. For the most part, the media treated me
with consideration—even with affection—both in my country and throughout the world.

In the Spanish newspapers, there was speculation
about the need for a bone marrow transplant. It was announced that a transplant would only be possible if the
right donor could be found. The foreign press picked up on
this, and soon people from all over the world were calling
the hospital or contacting my family to offer themselves as
donors. Some people actually went to see my doctors. Others wrote to me directly and said they were ready to drop
everything and travel to Barcelona if they could be of any
help. These letters were heart-warming, and the people
were obviously sincere. One of the volunteers, a woman
from Seville, was interviewed on a radio program along
with other potential donors. She said that she wasn't a fol-

lower of classical music or opera, but wanted to donate her bone marrow because "It would be a tragedy if such a famous Spaniard as Carreras were to die."

Finding the right donor is like finding the proverbial needle in the haystack. For a transplant to be successful, the tissue of the donor and the patient must be compatible. Compatibility is guaranteed only between identical twins; between siblings, it's chancy, between parent and child, it's a rarity. Finding the right donor takes time and money, but time is the biggest problem since the transplant should take place as soon as possible after the illness starts.

In my case, it was soon obvious that no one in the family qualified as an ideal donor. We couldn't count on using my brother, Alberto, or my sister, Maria Antonia; we couldn't use my half-brother, Jordi, or even my father. The doctors discovered that my son Alberto had the highest match—seventy-five percent—but even this was not considered good enough. Because of the expected complications, the odds made it too dangerous. You'd think that the body would accept any healthy new bone marrow, but the body isn't at all happy about foreign tissue. There's always the danger of rejection, which is why people sometimes don't survive the process.

For me, there was no choice: I would have to undergo a transplant in which my own cleansed bone marrow would be used. Over the next few weeks, the doctors would get me ready.

Overleaf.
As Alvaro, *La forza del destino*, the Met, 1983. I thought I was a happy man, giving my all to a lifestyle which consisted of circling the globe from performance to performance. But my destiny led me through a detour.

4

Preparing for Seattle

On August 24 I went back to the Hospital Clinico for a second chemotherapy treatment. It rained all day. My mood was as sullen and gloomy as the weather. I felt well enough to drive myself to the clinic, but even the pleasure of being behind the wheel wasn't enough to cheer me up. I was too painfully aware of all that was in store for me.

The doctors were optimistic and satisfied with the results of my second treatment. They had reacted in the same way after the first treatment, one month before. But for me a new problem was beginning: I was losing my hair.

One morning I held up a handful of hair and felt the shock of reality. Of course, the doctors had warned me that I'd lose body hair as one of the side-effects of chemotherapy. I didn't pay much attention at the time because I was concerned about a much more important matter, the possible loss of my voice. But day by day, as my whole appearance started to change, it became harder and harder to face myself in the mirror. I don't think it was a matter of vanity; rather, I had the frightening sensation that I was wearing the mask of a stranger. All of a sudden I couldn't identify with the person I thought I was. I felt uncomfortable with myself, at odds with this new image. It's an eerie feeling to look in the mirror and see someone else—someone you don't expect. Yet this someone is you, a victim of unpleasant emotions, turned inside out, bleak and bewildered. It's no wonder that you start feeling extremely depressed.

Even worse than the mirror is the way other people now begin to look at you, how they watch you and treat you. Some act tenderly. Others are pained when they see you this way. You feel their compassion, their pity, and sometimes even their disgust. That's when you want to cry and beg them, "Don't look at me like that! Does it really matter whether I'm handsome or not? I'm still me."

And then, as time goes by, there's a strange twist in your feelings. Your new appearance causes a fascinating reaction. You start to develop a sense of solidarity with your body and it gives you new energy to fight the disease. You don't want to give in. You want to fight to get back all that has been taken away: not only your health, but your former image, too. It's another challenge, to win back even the smallest bit of pride in your appearance. You resolve to do it, not so much for others, but for *yourself*.

This became my new goal.

By the time the sessions of the second chemotherapy treatment were over, we made the decision to have the transplant done in the United States. There were several reasons for it. The Fred Hutchinson Institute in Seattle is known as the foremost cancer clinic in the world. It was there, in 1975, that doctors performed the first bone marrow transplant. Since then more than 2,400 operations have taken place at the Institute. If the transplant were performed in Barcelona, the necessary radiation treatments would take place in one hospital and treatment for the bone marrow in another. Furthermore, Professor Rozman thought it would be better for me to escape from the journalistic turmoil I was experiencing at home, that my recuperation would be more peaceful in the United States.

It was also decided that Dr. Alberto Grañena, a physician from Barcelona, would come with me to the Hutchinson Institute. Dr. Grañena had already been to Seattle to study the transplant technique, and he would later be the first to use the procedure in Barcelona. I found it comforting to know that he would be with me, along with my sister and my brother, on the trip to the States.

On October 22, the final preparatory treatment began, one last chemotherapy session at the Hospital Clinico. Nine days later, on October 31, I left Barcelona for America. I started this trip with mixed emotions. For the most part, I was full of confidence. But something happened to cast a shadow on my last day at home. I didn't see it as a bad omen, but it affected me deeply: we had to put our beloved German shepherd, Lido, to sleep. The whole episode was very depressing, especially to my children, and I found it difficult to leave them while they were so unhappy. I knew that I'd be gone for many, many months.

Of course, Alberto and Julia didn't suspect that if things didn't go well for me this might be our last good-bye.

As Puccini's Rodolfo, my first time in San Francisco, 1973. Seattle is up the coast, but I had no premonition about it.

5

The Bone Marrow Transplant

U<small>NTIL</small> I arrived in Seattle, I knew little about the city except that it is situated in the State of Washington and is the birthplace of the Boeing jet. It's also home to a remarkable opera company.

Often referred to as the American Bayreuth, Seattle is a leader in presenting the music of Richard Wagner. The Pacific Northwest Wagner Festival is unique in that it offers *Der Ring des Nibelungen* in both English and German during the same summer season, an extraordinary achievement and a matter of pride for the festival management. I had only performed in Seattle once, in an evening of *Lieder* in 1978.

Although I'd heard of the Fred Hutchinson Cancer Research Center, I knew very little about this impressive hospital. Affectionately called "The Hutch" by members of the scientific community, this hospital has the reputation of being the best leukemia clinic in the world, and I was soon to find out why. It didn't take me long to discover the dedication of the doctors and nurses and to appreciate the personal care the staff gives each patient.

When I passed through the doors of the Hutchinson Institute I walked into a world of medicine so coldly uncompromising that it takes a European by surprise. At first it was the directness of the doctor-patient interaction that was such a shock. Europeans are not accustomed to having their doctors discuss things so factually, or, to put it bluntly, so cold-bloodedly. European doctors have a tendency to go easy on their patients, to soft-pedal the really bad news; they keep their suspicions to themselves and make a final diagnosis only when there's no chance of a mistake. Yet whenever an American physician finds something suspect in an X-ray or blood test, his usual bedside manner is to let the patient know everything, all the dire ramifications and morbid interpretations. He then promises to order more tests just to be sure. Meantime, the patient is on tenderhooks. Luckily, this happened to me only once; but once was enough. After spending a sleepless night, tossing and turning over all the alarming possibilities, I was told not to worry and that everything was going to be fine.

As I was introduced to the daily routine at the Hutch, another unexpected oddity was the number of signatures required. It was absolutely bizarre. Every medication, every injection, every prescribed bit of attention needed a signature. It wouldn't have surprised me if someone had asked for my signature to wish me "Goodnight." One day I teased a woman doctor about that. I told her it was easier to sign a contract with the Met than to get a suppository in an American hospital! Now I know that American physicians do this to protect themselves against malpractice claims. Signing releases before certain treatments is accepted behaviour.

All in all, I was impressed with the organization and management of the Hutch. Entrance procedures begin with a complete run-down of the patient's history and include a preview of the diagnostic examinations and proposed therapy. The pain and stress that each patient will have to face is discussed honestly and up front. In this case, I appreciated the doctors' habit of being straightforward. They gave me fair warning of what lay ahead. There were to be no surprises, and I could steel myself for anything.

When an out-of-town patient is admitted to the Hutch, the management helps the family locate an apartment nearby. Family members are allowed to visit the entire day at the hospital and may even spend the night near the patient if they want, but proof of rental is required of anyone who doesn't live in the area. Having your family close by creates a familiar environment, which is especially important for the children, since it helps them overcome the emotional problems caused by a long hospital stay.

It affected me greatly to see so many little ones sick with leukemia, and I started wondering how I could help. I told myself, "If you get out of this alive, you'll have to do something." The suffering I saw around me gave me the idea to one day create the José Carreras International Foundation Against Leukemia.

I was admitted to the Hutch in November 1987. For the next four months, my brother rented an attractive apartment for the family, but until my release in February, I visited there only occasionally. My room at the hospital had a small anteroom that was large enough for someone to sleep in overnight. The schedule my family adopted for my sake in Barcelona continued so that, even in Seattle, someone was always at my bedside—Marisa my sister-in-law, Ramiro my brother-in-law, and mostly Maria Antonia, my sister. It was decided that my sister would be the one to stay with me while I was hospitalized in America. The dedication with which Maria accepted this duty over so many months, and the tenderness she showed me day in and day out, touched me deeply.

As for the treatments I'd receive at the Hutch, the sequence was to be simple enough. First, my bone marrow would be extracted; then I would be given chemotherapy and radiation; finally there would be the transplant, or the reinjection of my bone marrow. Listing the sequence of procedures like this makes it all sound so easy. Yet I think of it now as a prescription for torture. For a leukemia patient, each step involves a great deal of torment, physical and mental. With each excruciating treatment, there is tension and anxiety. You keep wondering, "Will it work?"

Since we couldn't find a suitable donor for the bone marrow I needed, my only recourse was an autologous transplant in which my own rejuvenated bone marrow would be used.

The first step was to extract a little more than a quart of my own bone marrow. The procedure, orchestrated by the Clinic Chief of Staff, Dr. Donnall Thomas, began on November 6. (Dr. Thomas had performed the world's first bone marrow transplant at the Hutch in 1956.) Dr. Jean Sanders and my countryman, Dr. Grañena, performed the actual operation. To remove the bone marrow, the doctors made several hundred punctures into my pelvis. Once the bone marrow, a bloody, fat-containing fluid, had been extracted, it was sent to the laboratory to be cleansed of any cancerous cells. Then the marrow was frozen until it was needed again.

While Dr. Sanders and Dr. Grañena were performing the extraction, I had the oddest sensation. It was as if, there in the operating room, I was watching them tear out my life. "Without that bone marrow," I told myself, "I can't live." Because I was under local anesthesia, I didn't feel anything at the time. But for weeks afterwards, the pain was intense, absolutely excruciating. No matter what position I took, my whole body ached. And there was no time to recuperate because immediately after my bone marrow was extracted I started into chemotherapy, a treatment that only added to the trauma and pain.

The days that followed were brutally drastic, everything in me was being annihilated. Aggressive cytostatic agents, poisons that attack the body's cells, are administered in doses that far exceed the limits of human tolerance. No one could survive these injections outside the hospital and without constant medical supervision. Initially, the poisons work to stop the development of cancerous cells in the bone marrow; then they attack and totally destroy the blood-forming marrow itself.

As if the follow-up chemotherapy is not enough torture, radiation therapy is given as a parallel treatment. So in addition to being poisoned, I was subjected to twenty-minute gamma radiations three times a day for five successive days. While under the gamma rays, I didn't feel or notice anything unusual. The terrible, painful side-effects came later. I felt perfectly wretched. I could hardly move because of the puncture wounds through which my bone marrow had been pulled out, and I was constantly nauseated. I barely had time to recuperate a little from one radiation exposure before they would wheel me in for another session of what I came to think of as my personal Chernobyl.

The patient assumes different positions under radiation. Each twenty-minute session seems to last forever. Because there was no clock in the room to watch the minutes crawl by, I devised my own unique way to measure time. Quietly, and sometimes just mentally, I would hum an aria from *La Bohème*, *Aida*, *Turandot*, or *La Gioconda*. After all, every tenor knows exactly how many minutes it takes to sing "Che gelida manina," "Celeste Aida, "Nessun dorma" or "Cielo e mar."

By simply adding up the minutes for each aria, I could predict quite precisely when each torture session would end. Once in a while a nurse would surprise me. This, I suppose, meant only one thing; since the nurses never subtracted one second from the radiation schedule, I must have been following a conductor who liked a slower tempo.

I could hardly wait for my "Zero Hour." "Day Zero" is the day of the transplant, when the doctors finally thaw and reinject your extracted bone marrow, now that your own body has tested free of cancerous cells. The scheduled time for the operation is known as the "Zero Hour." Counting down the minutes and days is commonplace at the Hutch. My countdown ended on November 16, exactly ten days after the procedure was started, with Dr. Sanders performing the injection.

No matter how many times this procedure has been explained to me, I'll never understand it. It's a mystery of nature: the thawed marrow isn't put back into your bones at all; it is simply injected into one spot—a vein. From there it travels through the bloodstream, miraculously and automatically finding its way into the empty bone chambers.

Once the injection is over, there's nothing to do but wait. And hope! "Will the new bone marrow 'take'?" Everything is precarious, you see, because the treatments before the transplant are so destructive. All of my remaining bone marrow and blood-producing cells had been destroyed, and, of course, my immune system was shut down, leaving me totally defenseless. At this crucial point, everything depended on whether or not my new bone marrow would become "combative." Unfortunately, it takes three to six weeks to find out because the marrow needs this much time to start reproducing blood cells. Until then all you can do is trust and hope, hope and trust.

This waiting period is critical, and many patients don't survive it; they fall prey to the smallest virus or bacterial infection. This is why I was transferred to the "LAF (laminar air flow) Room"—a highly disinfected area where everyone wears a face mask and where the patient's bed is encased in and protected by see-through plastic curtains.

This plastic drapery is unique in that it has built-in arm-length gloves used by the nurses to give us food and medicine. But the most wonderful thing about these curtains-with-arms is that they make it possible for people to touch you. (This is especially important for children and their parents.) It's terrible to have to spend weeks barricaded in such a small sterile area. It's such a comfort to be touched, stroked, or caressed. Just to be able to hold someone's hand can do miracles. Still, even allowing for all this, human beings have the capacity to endure almost anything, and this experience in the LAF room made me realize the tremendous inner strength that we only discover and mobilize when needed.

While waiting for my transplant to take, I received regular blood transfusions. The doctors hoped the platelets would step up the ability of my own blood to coagulate and avoid the danger of a hemorrhage. These many transfusions, as well as every other injection I needed, were given through an invention called the Hickman Line. The Hickman Line is a central vein catheter now used in hospitals all over the world, originally developed at the Hutch. It consists of a thin tube inserted through the jugular or subclavian vein close to the heart; positioned at the start of the therapy, it is not taken out until the treatment is over. Medication, anesthesia, and nutrients can all be supplied through the tube and quickly absorbed into the bloodstream, while, conversely, blood samples can be easily taken. When you consider that every day I had to have six blood tests, if it hadn't been for the Hickman Line the veins in my arms would have been torn to pieces in only a few weeks. It was Dr. Hickman himself who inserted my line in November 1987, and it was not removed until May 1988.

Because I couldn't eat for over three months, intravenous feedings through the Hickman Line were a part of my daily life. One of the ugly results of chemotherapy and radiation is a violent fungus infection that spreads inside the throat and mouth; the entire mucus area becomes raw and inflamed, covered with countless small blisters. As these blisters burst and bleed, the pain is unbearable, and swallowing is impossible. I was obsessed with worry during this period: what was this doing to my vocal cords? Were they being permanently scarred? It would be months before I'd know.

Even when the infections in my mouth and throat cleared up, I still couldn't eat. For three months in a row, my stomach rejected everything. Nothing would stay down, not even a sip of water. The Hickman Line literally kept me alive. Its highly concentrated intravenous feedings kept me going—but there was a dramatic change in my physical appearance: I soon began to look puffy, like a fattened calf.

The days crept by. Whenever I felt up to it, I'd call my children, and in my mind's eye I'd escape to Spain and look in on what was happening in their lives. I also tried to pass the time by listening to records and videos. For me, music has the power to soothe both body and soul, to soften the harshness of reality. Strangely enough, it was not an opera recording that captivated me and held my attention. Much to my own surprise, my favourite was the Piano Concerto No. 2 by Serge Rachmaninoff. I don't know why I was so mesmerized by this particular piece, but there were days when I played the record over and over, for hours on end. My brother and sister didn't say a word to me about this, but they probably thought I was losing touch with reality.

I turned 41 while in the Hutch. Considering the alternative, having a birthday in the hospital is better than having no birthday at all. Actually, it turned out to be a really happy day. I was deluged with congratulations—absolutely thousands of letters, cards, and gifts. The flood of mail and packages that started on my birthday didn't stop until well after Christmas; by that time the hospital personnel announced they were on the verge of postal collapse.

Every day my brother Alberto lugged in two trunks filled with gifts and put them next to the Christmas tree. We finally had to ask the post office to separate the letters from the packages, which helped us to save space and make sure nothing was lost. In all, one hundred and fifty thousand pieces of mail arrived. Oddly enough, one letter made it all the way to my bedside with only two words scrawled on the envelope: "Tenor, Seattle." It was from a Spanish fan living in Virginia.

Letters poured in from all over the world: America, Mexico, United Kingdom, Taiwan, Australia, New Zealand, Chile, Argentina, Canada, Japan, Germany, Austria, Italy, Russia, and, of course, my beloved Spain. I heard from fan clubs, from the nurses at the Hospital Clinico in Barcelona, from teachers and the children in classrooms, from total strangers, and naturally, from many, many of my colleagues. It was simply wonderful.

I must confess that a few of my colleagues' letters caused me to break down and cry. I not only heard from the famous stars, but also from those who perform the secondary or lesser roles. Everyone was generous and kind to me. My fellow tenors were especially gracious, including my presumably greatest rivals, Luciano Pavarotti and Placido Domingo. Luciano sent me a delightfully funny telegram: "José, get well. Otherwise, I won't have any competition!" He also called me long-distance several times and would typically punctuate our conversation by shouting "Forza campione!" into the phone.

During my long stay in the hospital, I'm happy to say Placido and I were able to completely reconcile our differences following our legendary dispute at a gala concert in Vienna, where we had disagreed over the order of appearance in the programme. We had already made peace; now we had the chance to cement a deeper friendship. Placido wrote me several letters, called me often, and even flew to Seattle to visit me. I've come to admire him, not only as a great artist, but as an extraordinary man.

This turn of events made me realize something: that what counts most is not the success we achieve as artists, no matter how prestigious it may be, but what we do for each other as human beings.

For the first few weeks after the transplant, I was uncomfortable, but I knew that I was getting better. Dr. Dean Buckner, a well-known oncologist at the Hutch, monitored my progress every step of the way, explaining the dangers that I still had to face, but building up my morale whenever I needed it. Finally, on December 23rd, Dr. Buckner allowed me to leave the clinic to spend Christmas at the apartment with my family and a few friends (among whom was Aquiles Garcia Tuero). I still had to return to the clinic every day for tests, but to spend a few nights away from the hospital bed was sheer pleasure!

While spending Christmas at the apartment, I managed to fend off the reporters who had flown in from Spain. I saw no reason for interviews or photographs. What could I tell them? I certainly didn't want to spend my few days out of the hospital talking about the terrible days I had had in the hospital and I still wasn't feeling well. After the exhausting treatments, I tired easily and was simply in no mood for coping with the demands of the press.

So we spent a truly quiet Christmas—a little television, a little listening to records, a little quiet fun.

We were relaxed and comfortable, and our mood was upbeat. We were all pleased with how well I was doing and optimistic about my recovery. Lucky for us, we had no idea that I would soon face a new crisis, the most dangerous since my bout with pneumonia in Barcelona. It happened as we turned the corner of the New Year.

Overleaf.
Revisiting Seattle. A televised press conference with Dr. E. Donnall Thomas, at the time director of the Clinical Research Division of the Hutch, and Dr. C. Dean Buckner, senior member of the Center's clinical research faculty. May 1989.

6

Death and Life

A LONG journey through a tunnel is the metaphor I use to describe those painful yet hopeful months that I spent in treatment, in Barcelona and Seattle. On some days the tunnel was well lit. On other days, it was dim. It might slowly grow brighter and brighter, and then, suddenly, there would be days of almost total blackout, and the darkness would come crushing down on me. But further ahead I could always see a small point of sunlight, beyond the gloom and past the shadows, a single, small flicker of hope. It was always there, even in the most terrible moments.

By the time Christmas of 1987 had come and gone, I thought I had at last left this tunnel that stretched into eternity. The first fourteen days after the transplant are considered the most critical, and I'd passed that point without a mishap. Dr. Buckner had assured us that everything was going well and that my body seemed to be rid of all leukemic cells. "The treatment is over," I told myself with a sigh of relief. All I needed to do now was to rebuild my strength little by little.

Then, in an instant, a total eclipse, the light in my tunnel was almost extinguished! Suddenly my new bone mar-

row became "paralyzed"; it had stopped regenerating
blood cells, and, consequently, my immune system had
shut down, leaving me defenseless. There was a reduction
of antibodies and it became clear to me that I was going
under. I had reached a dead end in the tunnel, and was
poised on the edge of an abyss.

No one seemed to know why my condition was getting
worse. Perhaps it was the slight cold I'd caught in early
January. Or perhaps some medication had interfered with
my bone marrow's regeneration process. I listened to all
the conjectures, but the "why" no longer seemed important. I knew that although I had put all my hope in science
and doctors, it was up to me psychologically to survive this
crisis.

"I can't let this happen," I kept hammering into my
head. I had suffered so much; I had done all that was asked
of me. I'd submitted to the hell of therapy and hadn't given
up. I would overcome this crisis too! But despite my deter-
mination, it was painfully clear to me that there wasn't a
thing I could do. My wanting to live, my will to fight, these
could not help me now. I was lying in bed, unable to lift a
finger in the battle. I was completely powerless.

Or was I? Would I be lost only if I let go of all hope, if I re-
signed myself to defeat? At the moment, I couldn't answer
this question. But one thing I knew for sure: I would never
give up of my own free will! Never. Once again, the thought
of my loved ones sustained me. I didn't want to lose them,
no matter what.

Medically, there was only one hope: GMCSF. These
five letters identify a drug that had been developed only a
year earlier by the oncology research team at the Hutch. In
layman's terms, GMCSF is an agent that activates the bone
marrow and gives it a "push" toward reproducing healthy
blood cells. My doctors in Barcelona knew that this drug

was being developed and tested in Seattle, and it was precisely one of the reasons why we had chosen the Hutchinson Institute for treatment. I know there are no miracles in medicine. But for me GMCSF was like a miracle, a gift from heaven and science in equal measure. The doctors gave it to me and it worked! My bone marrow was reactivated.

Once again, my family was my strength. Their affection and encouragement was an efficient medicine during those days of uncertainty. No matter how devoted a hospital staff is, to have someone you love near you is a very special help. (This tremendous supportiveness, so indispensable for adults, is even more life giving to the children.)

The doctors did all they could to keep my spirits up. Dr. Rozman gave me shots of optimism. He often called me from Barcelona just to tell me not to worry, which helped me enormously. And Dr. Grañena flew back to Seattle in mid-January to offer his medical opinion and to give me moral support.

Unfortunately, at the time that my bone marrow stopped regenerating, a smaller problem was added to this bigger one. It was less dramatic, but no less unpleasant. Three small polyps developed in my esophagus, which caused me much pain and made swallowing pure torture.

To swallow! A healthy person can't imagine what it's like to go for months without this basic function, not being able to eat anything solid, having very little, if anything at all, to drink. As I mentioned before, chemotherapy and radiation ruin the digestive tract, so it's impossible to keep anything down. The stomach and the intestines simply refuse to work. To compound this problem, swallowing itself sometimes causes unbearable pain.

It was then that I understood one of the paradoxes of modern medicine. Research has given doctors the power to cure some really complex medical problems. They have sophisticated equipment and many surprising possibilities with new therapies it their fingertips. What throws them off are the little problems! Basic, simple problems—such as finding a way for a patient to eat normally.

Dr. Grañena was the one who finally solved my difficulty, and the solution was absurdly simple. He brought me some Librax and Bellargal from Spain; these are brand names of relaxants that have been sold in pharmacies for decades, preparations that worked for me like a charm. (This might not, of course, be the answer for everyone.)

Finally, after three months of intravenous feedings, I could eat a normal meal! I can remember the exact date: February 4, 1988—two days after I was released from the Hutch as an out-patient. Suddenly I had a craving for *pastine-in-brodo,* a kind of noodle soup. A few days later in our apartment, I watched Fritz, my secretary, who also happens to be a fabulous cook, prepare mozzarella with tomatoes and basil. At the moment I didn't think I'd be in the mood for such a dish, but I cleaned my plate!

Finally, I began the first phase of my convalescence. I was allowed to take walks, do some gymnastics, and go on short trips by car or motorboat. The weather was beautiful, contrary to the usual on the Pacific coast. A local saying that "It's summer in Washington when the rain gets warmer" proved false. Seattle's beautiful terrain and landscape amazed me, for within just a few miles there were untouched forests and snow-capped glaciers, large vineyards and bountiful fishing grounds. I even tried my hand at salmon fishing a few times, but I always ended up having to buy my salmon in a Seattle supermarket.

But generally, my way back to life started hesitantly. Even though I was growing stronger each day, I still felt weak and tired easily. At least once every day, I had to return to the Hutch for tests, and although I was staying in the apartment I was watched constantly. My family had to write careful reports for the doctors that covered everything I did: how long I slept, what I ate, the number of calories I consumed, and so on. My bone marrow was forming rather slowly, but, thank God, evenly. Dr. Buckner was satisfied with my progress and predicted that I'd be able to leave for home on schedule. That elusive, wonderful, long-awaited day approached steadily until it was finally within my reach.

On February 26th I left Seattle and the Hutch. My heart was filled with gratitude. The hospital staff expressed hundreds of good wishes, and complimented me for having been such a cooperative patient. As we drove to the airport, the countryside was picture-perfect, as if it were a gigantic photograph that had just dropped out of a beautifully illustrated book. I saw this as a sign that I was leaving behind one chapter in my life and starting another.

We flew non-stop to London and then, in a private plane, continued on to Barcelona. When, on February 27th, we finally touched down on Spanish soil, I had been away for 119 days.

Overleaf.
Top row: Drs. Alberto Grañena, C. Dean Buckner, Jordi Permanyer. Bottom: on my left is Dr. Cyril Rozman, and on my right, Dr. E. Donnall Thomas, the pioneer of bone marrow transplant, and Nobel prize winner (1990). I invited them to share my return to the international music scene: the September 16, 1988 recital at the Vienna Staatsoper.

7

Homecoming: Barcelona

My countrymen outdid themselves in planning a welcome for me. As my homecoming had been announced in the newspapers, crowds of fans had gathered at the Barcelona airport to give me a splendid and emotional reception. They waved banners inscribed with loving headlines and generally celebrated my return with applause, and shouts of encouragement.

As I stepped off the plane, I was surrounded by dozens of journalists and photographers. In fact, several newsmen had gone to the bother of going to Seattle a few days before just so they could fly back to Spain on the same aircraft with me. Well, the time had come to satisfy the media's insatiable curiosity, and since I had been making some plans I felt that I was ready to talk about the future, at least in broad terms. The thing to do under the circumstances was to hold a press conference. Naturally, the uppermost question in everyone's mind was when I would be returning to the stage.

All of this feverish commotion, this huge and concerted effort to welcome me, was quite tiring—yet I relished every single, exquisite minute of it. My state could best be described as happy exhaustion. And the best part of the day was still to come, seeing my children, Alberto and Julia, again. Our reunion was to be the greatest joy of all.

I was home, back where I belonged, beginning a new life. But one thing was absolutely clear: I could never go back to the kind of life I had before. Each hour, each minute had become far too precious to me. It had taken a devastating illness to make me realize the importance of certain things—things that are a self-evident truth and should be apparent at first glance. Unfortunately, most of us just don't take the time to think about the obvious. But to my mind, it's well worth our while to do so. Even the cliché, "You only live once" is not really trite. It's a statement that deserves our greatest respect and attention.

I knew it would be a while before I could pull myself together, as almost eight months of hospitalization are enough to change anybody. The trauma of continuous ups and downs and the anguish during treatment had taken their toll. I needed time to put my mind at ease and to restore my spirit. Above all, I needed a normal lifestyle to rediscover my serenity and my sense of humour. Meantime, I was trying to do my best to be a realist, to consider what was happening to me without euphoria and without exaggeration. Being level-headed was the best way for me to develop a cautious optimism. For the moment, that was enough.

I was out of the hospital, but not as yet through with hospitals. I continued as an out-patient at the Hospital Clinico for many weeks. All this time, I had to fight off a terrible desire to sing. It was a phantom wish that followed me everywhere. But, for the moment, I couldn't even think about it. The doctors had warned me to go very slowly, very carefully.

Yet it's impossible for me to sit still and do absolutely nothing. I took advantage of the time to accomplish other things. At this point, my decision to live a changed life-style almost went out the window. With unrestrained enthusiasm, I threw myself into creating the Foundation Against Leukemia. For some time, I had been nurturing the idea of such an organization, trying to think of the many ways it might help leukemia victims. I thought we might collaborate with hospitals specializing in the treatment of this disease. Or we could set up a system to help individual families with the enormous hospital bills. Perhaps, and I think this goal is the most valuable, we could work out a way to support research efforts.

One day, I am convinced, this dream will come true. Our new foundation will take its place in the international scheme of things and work with similar organizations all over the world. The Foundation's first commitment is to endow the Hospital Clinico with sufficient funds to install and outfit several sterile recovery rooms. These will be modeled after the LAF rooms at the Hutch.

For the last few months, I've made an all-out effort to publicize the José Carreras International Foundation. I've travelled extensively and spent a lot of time giving interviews. My hope is that if I can convince news people of how important the project is, and share my enthusiasm with them, they'll spread the word to their readers. While I was in Madrid, I visited Felipe Gonzales, our Prime Minister, and he agreed to serve as the Foundation's honorary president. I couldn't ask for greater support. For my own part, I've promised to give several benefit performances a year for the Foundation, reserving the right to direct the specific allocation of all the funds collected. Generally speaking, the money will be used to benefit a leukemia institution in the city where the concert is held.

In spite of all these activities I realized that I wasn't quite home yet. I was still standing in the wings offstage, so to speak, waiting for my return to the theatre. This business was first on my agenda, and soon after landing in Barcelona, something happened to spur me on; it was a happy and touching occasion.

Right about this time, Giordano's *Fedora* had its premiere at the Liceo; Renata Scotto and Placido Domingo were starring, and I decided to go to their second performance. The idea was irresistible: to walk again into an opera house after a year of forced rest, to sit in the audience, to smell the dust on the stage. I knew I'd have a wonderful evening; I had no way of knowing just how overwhelming it would be.

My long-time friend Lluis Andreu, the artistic director for the Liceo, reserved a box seat for me. I didn't want to attract attention, so I quietly took my seat in the dark just as the second act was beginning. It was a very handsome production. And everything happened as I knew it would. I relished the flavour of the theatre again, an atmosphere I was so used to breathing in: the expectant hush in the auditorium just before the conductor walks out, the applause to welcome him, the hush again as the curtain rises. Everything was just as I remembered. So natural, so predictable, yet, for me, each little happening was an experience.

Unbeknown to me, the rumour that I was in the audience—in "my" Liceo—travelled fast. It whispered its way to the actors on stage. And when the curtain came down at the end of the act, a delightful misunderstanding took place. It was just like Placido to want to welcome me and point me out to the audience. With that thought in mind, he stepped forward to the edge of the stage and searched the theatre with his eyes, but he couldn't pick me out of the crowd. We didn't connect for a very good reason. When the curtain came down, I had quickly left my box seat and gone backstage to congratulate everyone on their wonderful performances. So while Placido was straining his eyes to find me in the audience, I was standing on the stage right behind him, no more than two feet away, hidden by the curtain.

When Placido gave up looking for me, and returned backstage, he found me there, surrounded by Renata Scotto, Vicente Sardinero, and the other performers. We hugged each other, and then Placido quickly turned and went back in front of the curtain. Waving his arms, he caught the audience's attention. The theatre fell silent, and I heard Placido's voice: "This is a special moment, so I'm going to do something very unusual during this opera performance. It is a great joy for me to tell you that tonight we have with us a great friend, someone who is also a great glory of Spain: Josep Carreras."

At that point, when I least expected it, my colleagues walked me out onto the stage, and then to my surprise, every one of them just disappeared. They left me there alone. What a moment! The audience stood up, everyone at the same time, and the ovation that exploded was so moving I couldn't stop my tears. I felt that this show of jubilant affection was for Carreras, the man, not Carreras the tenor. The excitement seemed to go on forever. Flowers began to rain on the stage. I just stood there, unable to say or do anything for almost ten minutes. I could only think, "Some day, I will have to thank them for this moment." I will, I must, make it happen. It was a promise I made to myself.

Four months have gone by since that special "homecoming." And today, the 21st of July, is the day when I keep my promise.

Little by little it's getting darker and the Arch of

Triumph is festively lit. I've changed my clothes, and I'm totally concentrating on what lies ahead. One last word with Vincenzo, and we can begin.

While we're both anxiously watching the clock, we hear the applause. There are many cheers. These sounds come closer and closer, and we realize that Queen Sofia has arrived with her entourage. The applause is loud and intense. I think that there must be a lot of people out there, and I, too, want to be there with each and every one of them.

Well, this is it.

My wonderful day.

8

My Second Debut

It's a few minutes past ten in the evening—Carlos Caballé gives me one last hug—and I begin to make my way toward the grand piano. As I reach the steep gangplank leading up to the stage, I feel someone's lips on my right hand. It's Diego Monjo, bless him, the old prompter from the Liceo, my home theatre. Our affection is mutual, and his last-minute gesture touches me deeply.

Suddenly, the fiery brilliance of the spotlights envelopes me, and I move inside the gigantic halo across the stage and toward the piano. This is a walk of twenty-five seconds. But a flood of memories washes over me, and I can't do a thing to stop the flow. Wave after wave of fleeting images, brief, elusive scenes from my past—the difficult times in my early career; the shattering news that I had leukemia; the horrible night afterward as I wrestled with my fears; the sensation of being close to death. The hope. The agony of chemotherapy, a bitterly inhuman process; the bone marrow transplant; the fear and the endless waiting. The awful pain, and the fighting for my life. But most of all the hope, always there, always new. Could all of this have happened to me just last year? It seems an eternity ago.

I sense my feet moving toward the piano, but I feel as though I'm floating, spellbound by all that's around me. There is an ovation, the applause thunderous. Glancing out at the audience, I'm amazed. People, people, and still more people—as far as the eye can see. The entire park in front of the Arch is jammed, as well as the streets and alleys. I was told later the concert drew over one hundred and fifty thousand spectators. Perhaps "spectators" is the wrong term because the majority of the people had to stand so far away they couldn't even *see* the projection screens; they could only listen.

I keep on walking, as if in a trance, toward the piano. When I reach it, I suddenly realize that this is the crucial moment—the moment I've been bracing myself for. "Don't be an idiot," I tell myself. "Why do you think you're here? To cry? No . . . . To sing!" But right now, to sing would be impossible. I'm overwhelmed by the affection I feel streaming from the audience. My throat constricts; I'm choked with emotion. The applause goes on. It is, I think, the longest I've ever experienced. For that I'm grateful. It gives me time to get hold of myself. I stand looking out at the audience, and, slowly, one face after another comes into focus. I see Her Majesty, Queen Sofia, in the first row; sitting next to her is my good friend Narcis Serra, the Minister of Defense. And there is Jorge Semprun, the newly-appointed Minister of Culture, and Javier Solana, the Minister of Education. Looking further, I find Jordi Pujol, the president of Catalonia, and Pasqual Maragall, the Mayor of Barcelona. And finally, I see my whole family, especially my children. Their faces are glowing with excitement.

Slowly the applause dies down. I hesitate; should I say something now? No, I decide to wait until later.

I nod to Vincenzo, and the concert begins.

For my first song, I have chosen "T'estimo," a Catalan

adaptation of "I love thee," by Grieg. I wanted to open this concert with a very personal song, one in which each person could hear me say "Thank you for believing in me. Thank you for being afraid with me. Thank you for helping me in your own special way." No other song could express my feelings more deeply or with more sincerity. The song takes only a few minutes, but I give it my all.

I hear shouts of "Bravo!" Again, there's a tremendous roar of applause, and I savour the sound, drink it in, enjoy it more than I ever have before. It reverberates in huge waves, ebbing and flowing through the mass of spectators and the immense space around the Arch of Triumph, blending and resounding, and I imagine it absorbing even the last clap of hands in a faraway alley. I feel exhilarated. Stupendously so. Yes, applause is essential for performers; we need it as much as the air we breathe.

Finally, I reach the point where I'm in control and can trust myself to speak. I thank my compatriots—in Catalan, our mother tongue—for being here with me tonight. Then, in Castilian, I salute the Queen. For the past year, Queen Sofia and King Juan Carlos have followed my progress, and it has meant a great deal to me to have the royal family show such concern. Their gracious telegrams were always elegantly reserved in tone, but still very pleasant and friendly. Tonight, I'm greatly honored that Her Majesty has flown here from Madrid to attend my comeback performance.

My opening remarks are over, and I find myself relaxing. Once again I begin to feel at home on the stage. This is where I belong.

Now that my nervousness is almost gone, I can focus on my singing. With each song, I feel more sure of myself. I never knew I could feel so fantastically happy and after the next song, even happier. I suddenly realize that for me, singing is a physical, sensuous pleasure. I taste each note, each phrase. And at this moment, I hope the audience is drinking in my performance with this same intense delight. I think they are! The atmosphere is charged. Bursts of applause shatter the air whenever I sing a Catalan song or a fragment from a *zarzuela*. Every time the audience shouts "Bravo!" or calls my name, I feel I'm part of a football game and I've just scored another goal.

When I take my offstage breaks, Carlos asks me if I'm surprised that so many more people than we had expected have come to the concert. I'm astounded at the turnout, too, but I think I can explain it. First, the opera lovers were sure to come. They're here because they were afraid they'd never hear me in a live performance again. I also think we attracted a lot of people who don't regularly follow the opera, but who happened to follow my story in the news. They see me as someone who won out over a terminal illness and its ghastly treatment. I can imagine they're thinking, "This man fought to live. He worked hard to achieve this comeback, and here he is, singing for us tonight!" They wanted to witness the wonderful ending to my story. But, most of all, it's my fellow Catalans who are here—in droves. I know my people. They're happy I am giving my first recital in Barcelona and that they have the chance to hear me before anyone else. They know this performance is my gift to them, and they are pleased. Several times, during interviews with the press, I vowed, "If one day I return to the stage, my first appearance will be at home in Barcelona." Tonight the Catalans can see that Carreras keeps his word.

What I only dared to hope has at last become reality. The recital is almost over, and everything has gone well. Tonight I am the happiest man on earth. Just as I had so carefully selected my first song, it is not by chance that "Nessun dorma" will be my last.

In the literature of opera, it is easy to find a passage that expresses a particular idea or a special feeling; the story and the setting may be different, but the analogy is there. This *romanza* is from *Turandot* by Puccini. I feel a kinship with Prince Calaf, especially when he sings the finale, "Vinceró!" "I will win! I will win! *I will win!*" Even as Calaf sings these words, he knows his fate lies with Princess Turandot, a cruel and dangerous woman. He matches wits against her in a life-or-death contest, but all the while he is confident that luck is on his side and that he will win. With my "Vinceró" I want to say that I identify with Calaf. I never gave up hope of coming through my ordeal alive, and I now face the future with confidence. I'll do what must be done; I will not let myself be intimidated.

My second debut has come to a close. The ovation begins, and suddenly Montserrat Caballé is on the stage next to me, just as she was after my first debut, years ago. We kiss and hug while the audience goes wild. Montserrat hands me a giant heart-shaped bouquet made up of hundreds of roses. Vincenzo doesn't leave me any time to get emotional, but strikes the keyboard—a cue that Montserrat and I should seal the evening with a special encore: the drinking song from *La traviata.* I ask the audience to sing along and take the part of the chorus; they do so with obvious delight. Queen Sofia is the first to join in.

What a day this has been! An absolutely wonderful day for me! Now that the concert is over, the whole place is in a turmoil. The area around the stage has been cordoned off by the police, but nothing can keep the people from pouring through. Everyone wants to congratulate me. People I've never seen before throw their arms around me, slap me on the back, squeeze my hand. Microphones are pushed in my face; television lights flare.

Everyone is talking and shouting at the same time. It is utter chaos and I love every minute of it.

My brother, Alberto, is the first one in the family to reach me. He gives me a wordless hug. What is there to say? At times like this, words only get in the way. My sister, Maria Antonia, and I also seal the moment with a strong, silent embrace. Everyone is here: my wife; my son and daughter; my father; my other brother, Jordi; my sister-and brother-in-law, Marisa and Ramiro; and my wife's family. My daughter Julia is beaming. She says that when she handed a bouquet of flowers to the Queen, Her Majesty kissed her on the cheek.

My son, Alberto, is laughing: he claims he has come up with a good name for the German shepherd puppy Uncle Nino brought us this morning. After hearing my rendition of "Vinceró," he thinks that we should call our new dog "Calaf." So right then and there, we all get into a big discussion over what to name the pup. It may sound strange that at this moment a dog's name should be so important to us, but this is typical of our family. Finally, I decide that the dog—such a tiny thing—should be called "Petit," which is Catalan for "small." Of course I had no idea that Petit would in no time at all grow to be much larger than our other German shepherd.

All the while, the bedlam continues. The crazy frenzy lasts for almost an hour and a half, and although I'm exhausted I enjoy every minute of it. What's more, I still have our family celebration to look forward to. It's going to be exactly what I wanted. We'll all go home for a Catalan dinner, and the menu will be my favourite: *pa amb tomaquet i pernil*, bread with tomato and ham. And best of all, Fritz, my secretary, is footing the bill for the gigantic ham. Fritz should know better than to bet against me, as he did. He didn't think I'd be ready to perform until autumn.

But we're not home yet. I don't know how we'll ever manage to break away from here. The place is a madhouse, and I am boxed in by thousands of people. Somehow, some-way, someone pushes me into my car. What I see next is the biggest surprise of this whole unforgettable evening. Along both sides of the street, there is a solid wall of people, thousands of people. They have been standing and waiting all this time. I start the motor and begin to drive slowly, very carefully through the crowd. All the while I'm bombarded by cheers and a strong, steady chant: "José! José!" At the end of the street, just as I begin to accelerate, several dozen people break away from the crowd to race after my car, still shouting my name and waving at me.

This is all very moving, and I realize, once again, what is so marvelous about my profession. An opera singer loves to sing; and, yes, singing itself is enough to make us happy. But what's even more wonderful is that we can bring happi-ness to those who come to hear us. I can't think of anything else that would be so rewarding. I sing to bring joy to others.

How does one become an opera singer? There's no one formula. I can only tell you what happened to me.

As Nemorino, in *L'elisir d'amore,* San Francisco, 1975.

9

Childhood and Opera

M Y CHILDHOOD was happy and totally care-
free. Many things I remember clearly. Many important
family events or funny situations that happened when I was
very young, I know from stories which, as happens in many
families, have been told and retold over the years.

I was not yet five years old when my parents decided to
leave Spain and emigrate to Argentina. They left in search
of a new and better life because, at the time, Spain was eco-
nomically devastated. Although the terrible Civil War had
been over for twelve years, our country had not yet recovered, and the average Spanish wage earner in the late 1940s
was bringing home less money than his counterpart fifty
years before and only half as much as before the war
started. Since the economy showed no promise of getting
any better, many Spaniards just pulled up stakes and left
the country.

Our family had political reasons, too, for wanting to
leave Catalonia. Like most Catalans, my father, Josep Carreras-Soler, had fought in the Civil War and had passion-
ately defended the Republican cause. He was a young man,
only twenty-three years old when he fought at the front. He
came back alive and unhurt. But he was ruined profession-

ally. Before the war my father had been a teacher of French; when the war was over he was no longer able to find employment. It soon became obvious to him that the Franco government would never allow a Republican to teach in their schools. Of course, nothing was officially said; that is, my father was never told by the school administrators that they wouldn't hire him because of his political beliefs. In those days, all someone had to say was, "We're sorry, there's no opening."

As an alternative, my father tried to find a position with the city government, but no one was needed there either. Instead, he was offered a job with the traffic police, which, out of desperation, he accepted. I don't have to explain what it means for a man who loves teaching children to find himself on a street corner directing traffic. But he had to earn a living; after all, he was the young head of a family. He and my mother had married during the war, and Alberto had been born in 1937. Creating a home during the postwar years was a real economic struggle and, most likely, it was the reason that my sister and I were born several years later, Maria Antonia in July 1942 and I on December 5, 1946.

My mother, Antonia Coll-Saigi, was always the driving force of the Carreras family, a fantastic woman brimming with energy, vitality, and imagination. Being thrifty and independent, she ran a small hairdresser's shop and her earnings contributed greatly to the household. Of course, at that time there were people in Spain who were poorer than our family, but my parents couldn't resign themselves to this situation. It was my mother's brother who kept encouraging them to leave Spain. He had gone to Argentina two years before, and his letters had always spoken of the advantages that South America had to offer.

After many long discussions, my parents decided to

take the chance, and in the autumn of 1951 we said goodbye to our homeland, Catalonia. My mother's parents went to Argentina with us, but my paternal grandparents remained in Gerona, their native city. Once in Argentina, my parents quickly understood that their dream of a better life would not be realized there. First, the family sublet an apartment from my uncle in Villaballester, but after a short time in these narrow and confined quarters, we found our own place in José Leon Suarez, a small town near Buenos Aires. The next few months proved how hard it would be to gain a foothold in Argentina. My mother found work as a hairdresser, but there was no demand for my father's services, since teaching vacancies were nonexistent. His only recourse was to accept a variety of odd jobs that came his way. Our living conditions were bleak, so it was with relief rather than sorrow, that the family council made another decision, to go back home to Spain.

The odyssey in search for a new life lasted eleven months, but the only real memory I have of this time is of crossing the ocean. I was a fun-loving kid, full of mischief, and I entertained myself and the rest of the passengers on board ship with tricks and jokes. I did a little singing and dancing, and even an imitation of the adults doing the tango. Soon I became a shipboard attraction, and the passengers spoiled me with sweets and coins. Oh yes, it definitely was a pleasure cruise for me!

Many years later, I returned to Argentina, when I gave a concert with Agnes Baltsa in the fall of 1986 at the Teatro Colon in Buenos Aires. My cousin, José Coll, was kind enough to drive me around the country, and in a few days he reintroduced me to the cities of my childhood. It was just enough time to get an impression of the country and its people, a country which, for a short time in my life, we called home.

Our family's eleven months in Argentina gave me another asset in life: I learned Spanish! If you're not from Spain, this may sound strange, but it can be easily explained. Catalonia is a Spanish province, but we Catalans have our own culture and our own language. Most people think we speak a Spanish dialect, but we don't, really.

Today, thank God, Catalonia is an autonomous region. In fact, when Spain became a monarchy in 1976, Catalan was recognized as the nation's second official language. This means, for instance, that I'm now allowed to have my first name, Josep, written in its Catalan form on my passport. My full name is actually Josep Maria Carreras-Coll since it's customary to use our father's family name along with our mother's. When I was a child, the official language of Spain was Castilian, even though one-fourth of Spain's population spoke Catalan as their mother tongue; today, the percentage is still the same. As children, we spoke Catalan at home, and it was only when we went to school that we heard Castilian. I was lucky that during our stay in Argentina, I had learned to speak Spanish because when I went to school in Catalonia, I had a big advantage over the other children.

As proverbs go, Prussians are very exacting, and Spaniards are very proud. "Proud as a Spaniard" may be a common saying, but it's even more applicable to those of us from Catalonia. Spain's long-awaited resolution of Catalonia's autonomy has made me very happy for a special, somewhat psychological, reason. Now that the state allows me to carry papers identifying me as a Catalan, it's wonderful to be a Spaniard. It's that simple! My parents also dreamed of this day, but, in the early 1950s, it didn't seem likely that Spain would ever recognize us as a separate people.

In the summer of 1952, when our family returned to Barcelona, the economy had not improved and neither had the political scene. There was still no job for José Carreras-Soler, the teacher, but since my father had only asked for a leave of absence when he sailed for Argentina, he could at least return to his old job as a traffic policeman. I believe it was about this time that my father abandoned all hope of ever practicing his chosen profession. But for us, his children, he was forever the teacher. Since he knew that we were bringing home the ideologies taught in school, he made it a point of teaching us his own brand of liberalism. The cornerstone of his beliefs about education and our upbringing was "to think and act critically, but without prejudice." His lessons have served me well, and so today, as an adult, I wish to thank him.

When our family returned to Catalonia, our parents looked for a place to live, and they found what they wanted in Sants, a working-class suburb of Barcelona. Our new house, quite close to our old residence, was relatively large and rather expensive for those times. It was my mother's farsighted thinking that saved the day. She turned a section of the house into a hairdresser's shop, and the investment proved sound, even if at first the returns were modest. As for me, her salon became my first stage.

"How does one become an opera singer?" I'm frequently asked this question, but as I've said before, there's no single answer. A master formula or recipe to be an artist doesn't exist. Opera is not a profession one simply chooses and then begins to practice right away. For each person, the way is unique. With me, it had a lot to do with Enrico Caruso.

During countless interviews, I've mentioned how, as a young child, my parents took me to see the film *The Great Caruso* with Mario Lanza. This story angle is always brought up when someone writes about my career, but it's been misinterpreted so many times that I'd like to set the record straight. It's definitely stretching the truth to say that after seeing this film I decided to throw myself into an opera career to become the next Caruso. After all, I was only six years old when I saw this film, and my future plans were limited at best to the next few days, "Would I have time to play football with my friends?" Or "How many goals could I score?"

The film, however, did work its magic on me; it stirred up a desire I didn't know I had. It made me want to sing. In Spain during those years, films held an important place in people's lives since they were one of the few leisure activities that were affordable. Showtimes were Saturday and Sunday and you didn't pick and choose. You simply watched the film that was being shown that weekend.

The theatre in our neighborhood always had a double feature, so spending an afternoon there was great fun and somewhat of a curious event. People knew they were going to be at the theatre awhile, so they usually packed a lunch or brought along some refreshments. And spectators weren't exactly quiet for the whole show. In the middle of a steamy love scene, someone over in the corner might shout, "Pass the ham and cheese, will you?"; or you'd hear a child begging his parents for "Another soda, p-l-e-a-s-e . . . !" No one complained; people were having a good time, and the commotion was half expected. Yet, believe me, whenever there was a really dramatic moment on the screen, the tension could be felt throughout the audience; then you could hear a pin drop.

One day, the featured attraction was *The Great Caruso* and it was probably followed by a John Wayne western—I don't remember any more. Anyway, my parents took me along to see it, explaining that the movie was about the greatest tenor of all time, and that a "tenor" was "the singer who played the hero in an opera." It wasn't the story about Caruso that fascinated me. Of course, I noticed some of the details about his career, especially that he travelled a lot and became "famous" and "rich." But what really excited me about the film was the music—the arias and the way Mario Lanza sang them.

What happened the next day was definitely a shock for my family. Although I had never heard these arias before, I repeated all of them to perfection. And, more especially, I imitated the tenor's style of singing. After that, a difficult time began for my family because I sang and sang and sang. Finally they told me my singing was wonderful, but it was beginning to fray their nerves. So I started to look for places where I wouldn't bother anyone. As at this point I couldn't care less about a proper concert hall, I'd lock myself in the bathroom and sing in the shower for hours on end. Whenever I could find a quiet place by myself, I'd sing my lungs out. My favourite piece was the duke's aria, "La donna e mobile" from *Rigoletto*. No one has ever listened to that aria as often as my family. I was definitely struck by donna-mania!

When I was alone, I took my singing a step further. I'd use masks or clothes to dress up since I felt that my arias sounded much better when I was in costume. The day that I saw a magazine picture of Mario del Monaco as *Otello*, I knew that Otello would be my next project. Again and again, I tried to change myself into a black man by rubbing water colours on my face—until I thought I resembled the noble Moor. When my parents saw me, they weren't exactly thrilled, yet they couldn't help laughing behind my back. My brother and sister thought I was as mad as a hatter.

My parents had no particular interest in opera, and, anyway, they couldn't afford the luxury of going to the theatre very often. But they knew enough musically to understand that I wasn't singing in a childish way—that each note was correct and that I seemed to be musically gifted. Perhaps this talent had been inherited from my maternal grandfather, Salvador Coll. Blessed with a beautiful baritone voice, he had once wanted to be a singer. At first, he was the only one who showed any enthusiasm for my aria singing frenzy, and he did all he could to encourage me. My grandfather actually added fuel to the fire by telling me stories about the composers and describing all of the performances he had attended, both at the Liceo and at the Teatro Tivoli (which, unfortunately, has been torn down). Grandfather was a wonderful storyteller, and it delighted him that I could spend hours listening to his tales.

About this time, there was a popular singer in Spain, Luis Mariano, who sang arias from operettas, romanzi, and also some of the more ordinary songs. He was often heard on the radio and appeared in quite a few films. His movies were usually rather insipid—simple plots to showcase his songs. Yet, Mariano's voice and his type of music impressed me as much as had Mario Lanza's tenor and his famous arias. Naturally, I started imitating my new screen hero, not just repeating his songs, but taking on his whole style of acting, his gestures, his facial expressions, everything about him. I suppose it was all very comical, but my parents said they didn't know whether to laugh or to cry at the antics of their youngest child. At school I never passed up an opportunity to sing, so my schoolmates nicknamed me "Rigoletto." I don't think I need to explain why . . . .

One day something very important happened: our first record player appeared in our house. I didn't suspect it then, but the first record my parents bought would have an almost symbolic meaning later in my life. It was a recording of eight Neapolitan songs by Giuseppe Di Stefano. The second record was purchased especially for me—the original soundtrack of *The Great Caruso* with Mario Lanza.

Now I had a real opportunity to increase my repertoire, and I used the record player every chance I had. From this moment on, there was always someone singing in the Carreras home, either Di Stefano or Lanza, and they never sang alone. I was so spellbound I always accompanied them.

My new life as a tenor had also a practical side to it, which pleased me no end: pay for the "house soloist." In my mother's hairdresser's salon in our home, her customers would listen to my singing. They didn't have much choice, really. It seems, however, that the ladies were charmed by the hairdresser's "singing son," and they would often ask me to perform for them. With the tips they gave me, I bought Coca-Cola, ice cream, and other wonderful children's nonsense.

As for the rest, no matter how much my life was filled with singing, I still behaved like a normal boy. And what a wonderful time I had! The school was just across the street from our house, and, best of all, the sports field was there too. I spent hours playing football, handball, and basketball with my friends. As our school basketball team made it into the regionals, we all dreamed of becoming basketball stars. Even though I wasn't exactly known for being tall, I made the team. I retain happy memories of my playmates from those years, and two of them are still among my best friends: Miguel Sanroma and Josep Riba. As a matter of fact, Josep's mother, Magda Prunera, became my first piano teacher.

By now my mother had realized that singing was more than a passing fancy for me. On the other hand, she had no desire to push me or to advertise me as a child prodigy. Yet the belief in my talent prompted her to ask Josep's mother, who happened to teach music at the Orfeo in Sants, to listen

to me. Her friend agreed, though of course she was doubt-
ful; she knew how mother love can see things that aren't
there. In the end, however, my singing so delighted Mrs.
Prunera that she immediately took me under her wing.

A year later, I went to the Municipal Conservatory,
where my tuition was waived since father was a city policeman and considered a member of the local administration.
For the next three years, I immersed myself in music. And it
was at this time that I actually saw my first opera. I was eight
years old when this exciting adventure took place. My father, wearing his dress uniform, took me with him to Barcelona's famous Teatro del Liceo. I was resplendent in my
first Communion suit: a white shirt with tie, short grey
pants with a matching jacket, white socks, and black shoes.
It didn't matter that we had the highest seats in the house,
in the fifth and last gallery. The performance was *Aida*, with
Renata Tebaldi, who in that era was venerated in Barcelona
like a goddess. Umberto Borso sang Radames.

In every person's life, there are certain moments that
can never fade or die. For me that night was one of those occasions. I will never forget the first time I saw singers on a
stage and an orchestra. I admired the colourful sets and felt
the magic of the theatre all around me: the lights that dim
by degrees, the expectant silence until the conductor appears, the curtain that rises slowly, it was all very mysterious and fascinating.

When the curtain went down on *Aida,* the public called
for Tebaldi over and over, and each time she appeared to
bow I added my childish shouts to the ovations. As for the
opera itself, strange to say, I was more impressed by the
singing than by the spectacle of the Triumphal March, a
scene which should dazzle a child. Instead, I was completely enthralled by the Nile scene: Aida's aria "O patria
mia", her duet with Amonasro, and of course the following

confrontation between Aida and Radames at the edge of the river, its waters gilded by the reflection of the moon.

All this awakened a deep longing within me—yet I felt strange about what was happening. It was the first time in my life that I'd stepped into a theatre, but the place was as familiar to me as if I had always known it. At the time I couldn't understand my feeling. Today I can describe it this way: from the moment I crossed the threshold, I knew it was my world, I knew it was where I belonged. After that night and whenever we passed the Liceo by tram, I'd tell my parents: "Someday I'm going to sing in this theatre, for sure!" My parents were a little surprised at such confidence, but by now they started suspecting there was more to it than the wild dreams of an eight-year-old. The logical thing for me to have said would have been, "When I grow up I'm going to play center forward on the Barcelona football team!" If my parents were told then that their son would be on the stage of the Liceo just three years later, at the age of eleven, they'd have thought someone was pulling their legs.

But before this happened I gave my first public performance. It was Christmas, and the National Radio of Spain announced a benefit to collect funds for needy children. Many singers, actors, and musicians took part in the programme. I think it was Magda Prunera who suggested to my parents that I should appear, that it would be appropriate for a child to perform for other little kids.

The radio people loved the idea and invited me to be on the programme. I sang a Catalan Christmas carol and, not surprisingly, "La donna e mobile." The show had two hosts, one serious and the other comic. The first one introduced us while the second added a bit of humour. Mario Del Monaco was then singing *Otello* at the Liceo, and when it came my turn, the second announcer told the world, "If

Del Monaco falls ill or is unable to perform, we have here
the ideal stand-in." Of course, I was pleased as punch with
this introduction, and I put everything I had into my
pieces, especially Verdi (a recording of this radio programme is still treasured at home and has become a family
heirloom).

The aria from *Rigoletto* has really an impossible range
for a child. If I sang it in the *tessitura* of a tenor, it would be
too low. To sing it in the soprano's range wouldn't work
either because I was already too old for that. And so, I trans-
posed it. (I've often wondered at the fact that a boy with a
low voice usually becomes a tenor, while the boy with the
highest soprano evolves into a baritone.) Besides singing, I
had taken very seriously the chance to greet my family on
the air, and I made sure I sent a "Hello" to my relatives in
Gerona. When the broadcast ended, my family felt very
proud of me.

This appearance probably led to my next invitation to
sing. We never knew exactly how or why it happened, but a
few months later we received a phone call from a member of
the management of the Liceo. Would my parents let me appear at the theatre? The director wanted me to take the role
of a boy in an opera by one of our greatest composers, Manuel de Falla. My parents thought they were dreaming. It was
unbelievable, a real heart stopper.

You must realize that the Gran Teatro del Liceo was the
largest and most important opera house in Spain. And, in
addition, the de Falla evening would be rehearsed and conducted by no less than the world famous Spanish pianist
and conductor, José Iturbi. The family council convened
and it was agreed that the offer should be accepted.

Three works by de Falla were on the programme: *La
vida breve, El sombrero de tres picos,* and *El retablo de Maese
Pedro.* In the third piece, a boy explains all the scenes in a

marionette theatre to Don Quixote, and this was to be my part! Originally written for a soprano, it's a devilishly difficult part to sing. For over three months, I worked on the score with Magda Prunera, learning it as well as I could before I presented myself to Maestro Iturbi at the first rehearsal. Silently, he listened to me, and tears came to his eyes. From then on he treated me very warmly, and his praises and approval gave me the confidence I needed.

Opening night took place on January 3, 1958, a few weeks after my eleventh birthday. The performance was also on the radio and proved to be a resounding success. I had one moment of stage fright—not while I was singing, but when the baritone Manuel Ausensi took my hand and we walked in front of the curtain for our bows. When it was all over, I was paid my first professional salary, 500 pesetas. Nearly nothing, just enough to buy a small toy.

One other important thing happened to me that night: I gave my first interview. With a very serious expression, I told the reporter that I'd rather sing ten times at the Liceo than take one test in school. I didn't stop there. I also said that I preferred Verdi to Pythagoras and Puccini to Galileo.

My first contact with the famous opera house and the singers who performed there gave my parents a chance to seek advice about my future. Among others, they asked Maestro Iturbi if he saw a reasonable possibility of my becoming a singer. Don José's considered opinion was that it would all naturally depend on what happened when my voice changed—but he emphasized that in any event my musical talent was extraordinary and should be encouraged. He believed I was born to sing. This served to strengthen a similar idea my parents were already nurturing.

The day after the opening of de Falla's opera, I received my next offer from the Liceo. There was going to be a production of *Amunt* by the Spanish composer Manuel Altisent, and there was a part for a boy in it. I accepted, fulfilling this task successfully. Shortly after that I made my debut in my first Italian opera, *La Bohème*. As my appearance was limited to one phrase, "Vo'la tromba, il cavallin!" I wasn't overloaded with preparation. Those who love *La Bohème* know where this scene occurs. During the second act, a small boy is dragged from Parpignol's toy wagon. The boy's mother pulls him by the ear and the little fellow cries, begging for a trumpet and a wooden horse. Although years have passed, every time I sing Rodolfo, I take a good look at the boy by the toy seller's cart. Who knows? I may be listening to a future tenor!

For me the most exciting things about this performance of *La Bohème* were the stars: the same Renata Tebaldi whom I'd cheered a few years earlier from the fifth row of the balcony was standing next to me on the stage—even if it was just for an instant. And then there was Gianni Raimondi as Rodolfo. He graciously directed a few words to me, amiable, but probably insignificant for him, yet for me they were a great honour. Later, I convinced my family that the famous Raimondi was quite sure that I, too, would become a great tenor.

But that day was many years away. For now, my stage career ended abruptly. My voice was changing, and I had to decline an offer from the Liceo to sing in Humperdinck's *Hansel and Gretel* during the 1959-1960 season. My voice was out of control, doing whatever it pleased! Sometimes it sounded like Edita Gruberova's, and sometimes it resonated like Nicolai Ghiaurov's, certainly not in quality, but in tone, almost that high or that low! Naturally, I couldn't perform on the stage now but I kept on singing, which was the right move on my part as it's dangerous to stop singing while the voice is changing. And though my singing wasn't anything special at that time, my voice continued to evolve and develop in a completely natural way.

Between the ages of fourteen and seventeen, I didn't miss a chance to see performances at the Liceo. As a gift, my mother had bought me a Saturday subscription, and whenever possible I'd get a pass too. This was how I learned the traditional opera repertoire from Mozart to Wagner. At that time Wagnerian operas were performed in a mixture of languages: the soloists would sing in German while the chorus sang in Italian. As a teenager, I found it difficult to get excited about Wagner's music. The only work of his that inspired me was *The flying Dutchman*.

Rigoletto continued to be my favourite, and I attended every performance. My very first duke was the tenor Gianni Poggi. He trod the stage majestically, clad in an elegant costume, which he complemented with a pair of dazzling white gloves. As a boy I was completely overwhelmed when he'd slip his gloves off and caress them while singing his entrance aria, "Questa o quella." And all this time I continued to experience that strange, indefinable sensation: "You already know all this, you're at home here in the opera, this is your element since before time began."

My first serious training as a singer began in 1964. Barcelona was then in love with Giacomo Aragall. In my opinion, Giacomo possesses the most beautiful voice of our generation and at that time he was celebrating his first great successes in Italy. Everyone, everywhere was talking about him. What could be better than to study with the same singing teacher who had coached him? Aragall was, after all, a fellow Catalan. An audition was scheduled, and when Giacomo's teacher heard me he agreed to accept me as a student. The teacher's name was Francisco Puig.

A snapshot that turned out well caught me in a scene from *La traviata,* at the Vienna Staatsoper.

10

My Mother

I was to be a singer. It was all planned: everything I did, everything I thought, everything I touched moved me steadily and methodically closer to this dream. Nothing stood in my way.

Then, about a year after I began to study with Maestro Puig, tragedy struck our family; my mother died. Her death came as an unexpected blow. No one, not even she, suspected cancer. By the time the diagnosis was made, in the fall of 1965, her whole body was affected and the metastasis was complete. She was to live only ten days longer. When the end came she was just fifty-one years old. Our only consolation was that she didn't suffer too much or too long.

Four days before she died, Mother felt somewhat stronger, and we were able to talk. It was to be our last conversation, one that I will never forget. Those final moments with my mother defy description. She was interested in only one thing: my future—and I remember every word she said. She was absolutely sure that someday I would be a professional opera singer, and with a mother's tenderness she begged me to be careful, not to sing too much or take risks with my voice.

With all that has happened since the summer of 1987,

the words my mother spoke that day keep coming back. They haunt me with a new meaning. I don't believe in supernatural phenomena, and I don't consider myself to be particularly superstitious, but I wouldn't be surprised if my mother had a premonition that her youngest child would some day be a serious problem for the family. In fact, she made my brother and sister promise to keep an eye on me.

"I know that you will be someone very important." These were my mother's last words to me. I can still hear them. When your mother speaks like this on her deathbed, you never forget it. The moment, the words themselves, became a force in my life, and, as sentimental as it may sound, they continue to give me enormous strength. Whenever my need was the greatest, I derived courage and confidence from my mother's faith in me. I know that, over the years, remembering her has somehow helped me to get through many a difficult problem.

I owe my mother a great debt. I wish I could thank her for everything she did for me, especially for helping me to become the singer I am. And though I received the blessing and wholehearted support of my father, it was my mother who took the initiative and made the arrangements for my musical studies.

Besides all that, I'm indebted to my mother for saving me from certain death when I was two years old. She gave me life, not once but twice. I was too young to remember the incident myself, but I've been told the story many times since. During the 1940s, our family always spent three months each summer in Puigcerda, a small, picturesque town between Spain and France. It's an idyllic place where the French love to spend their vacations. My father worked for the Barcelona police, and because he was fluent in several languages, including French, he was regularly assigned to Puigcerda during the summer tourist season.

Mother took advantage of this to earn extra pin money as a hairdresser in Puigcerda. And, of course, we children went along.

One summer day, my two-year-old imagination caught sight of one of those small, now old-fashioned, aluminum shaving-cream containers, and decided it would be a perfect "ship" to sail in the nearby lake. Somehow I got my hands on it and wandered off to test whether it was seaworthy. I cast my little ship afloat, but when I tried to catch it and bring it back to shore, I fell headfirst into the water. Fortunately, someone saw what happened but by the time they pulled me out, I was unconscious. My mother was called, of course, but when she arrived my face had already turned several shades of blue. She sized up the situation and immediately gave me mouth-to-mouth resuscitation, breathing for me until I regained consciousness and started crying my heart out. Everyone was relieved. "Josep is in good shape!" But not so my poor mother. A delayed reaction set in, and it took her quite a while to get over the experience.

I must confess it was only when I was much older, and my mother had already been gone for many years, that I realized what a fabulous woman she was. Extremely sensitive, she had an uncanny maternal instinct that I couldn't understand then and still can't explain. Somehow, she always knew exactly what was best for each of her children. Her intuition was always on target. She was a rare woman: strong, but vulnerable; logical, but loving; strict, but also impulsive. And she was very forgiving. The most intriguing thing about Mother was that she had the right maternal response for each moment. I was only eighteen when she died, and at that age I wasn't mature enough to understand or appreciate all she did for us. I consider my older brother and sister lucky because they enjoyed more time with her.

Looking back over the years, I remember an amusing scene acted out many times over. I can still picture it. Once in a while, Alberto, who was a typical teenager, would come home late and find himself locked out. He'd start shouting from the street below, begging for someone to open the door. Then, from the window, Mother would play the heartless parent. She'd call down to Alberto that under no condition would she open the front door for him and that he better look elsewhere for a bed that night.

Their little game continued. Alberto threw pebbles against the window, while Mother remained completely unruffled. Then my sister and I would beg her to let the reveller in. For a while she'd pretend to have no mercy, and then, of course, she'd give in. We often reminisce and laugh about how Mother held "night court" at the window with Alberto.

In retrospect, I am convinced that if she had lived, my life would have followed a straighter path and I would have avoided certain mistakes and false steps. I suppose there's no perfect time to lose one's mother, but I felt mine left me when I needed her most. Suddenly, the protective hand was gone. This may seem too obvious to mention, even trite, but, for me, it was tragically true.

I felt a tremendous loss. Even though misfortune drew our family closer than it already was, and my father, brother and sister focused intensely on me, still everything felt different. Things had changed. I don't mean to say that after my mother's death I no longer knew what to do with my life. Absolutely not. I wasn't alone, and I wasn't overcome by despair. But I felt miserable. I missed that special place of refuge, that corner of her heart and mind where I could feel completely safe.

Despite this terrible loss, I held on to my firm desire to dedicate my life to a singing career. Only perhaps now I was somewhat careful and practical, deciding to enroll in the School of Chemistry at the University of Barcelona. This seemed to be a logical choice, since my brother, Alberto, and my sister's husband, Ramiro, had decided to go into business together and were just starting a cosmetic firm.

I began helping out in the new business, delivering supplies by car, running errands, and doing whatever I could in the way of odd jobs. No one asked me to do this. I just felt better contributing in some way. My family agreed with me on all counts. They thought it wise of me to learn another profession, but they still believed in my talent and my potential as an opera singer. So Alberto and Ramiro volunteered to pay for both my courses at the University of Barcelona and the singing lessons I continued to take.

As Riccardo, in *Un ballo in maschera*, Houston, Texas, 1981. I performed throughout the world, trying to live up to my old teacher's ideals.

11

Juan Ruax,
Teacher and Friend

F OR ALMOST three years, I took singing lessons from Maestro Puig. He was a very friendly, good-natured sort of man, a person of refined musical taste. As a teacher he had an excellent understanding of logical development in music. Yet a time came when somehow I felt I needed more, something he wasn't able to give me.

At this point in my life I wasn't sure of anything. And just then, with a stroke of good luck, I discovered Juan Ruax. He had been paralyzed since childhood and was bound to a wheelchair, but nature had been kind to him in another way: he had a fabulous tenor voice. Although it was a beautiful gift, he himself had never considered becoming a singer. Nor was he a professional voice teacher with the "proper" academic credentials.

Actually, Mr. Ruax was a dental technician.

In those days, we had a wonderful custom at parties and other social gatherings; we made music, playing and singing our favourite tunes. Juan Ruax often joined us in these get-togethers. After hearing me sing on several occasions, he took me aside at one party and said that if I really wanted

to become a professional opera singer he'd like to help. I
sensed right away that he had an instinct, a gift for this task.
He seemed to know at once exactly what was right and what
was wrong for my voice.

As a matter of fact, I'd been making some tentative
plans, but I didn't have a clear idea of where I should go.
Before Ruax made his generous offer, I thought I'd travel
to Italy and study voice there. After all, Italy had always
been a Mecca for young singers, and I was still a pilgrim.
Thank God, Ruax talked me out of this plan otherwise I'd
have missed his coaching and guidance.

I decided to stay in Barcelona and work with Maestro
Ruax. He was a simply wonderful man who totally dedicated himself to my career. Only much later did I learn that
he would start work at five each morning as a dental technician so as to have enough time to spend a couple of hours
with me in the afternoons.

He taught in a fascinating way: he spent more time talking about music than listening to my voice exercises. And
when I was singing, I must admit, he spent more effort on
teaching me how *not* to sing, than how to sing. Above all
else, he stressed the importance of my innate talent and my
natural instinct for singing, how important it was to simply
let these develop and bloom.

Of course, he handed out criticism and corrections
when I made mistakes, but the most important thing he
taught me was this, his one main principle: in singing, there
are no "basic" rules. You can't indiscriminately use the
same method with everyone because what works for one
singer might not work at all for another. Maestro Ruax always said there's no fool-proof singing method; if there
were, we'd have a world filled with first-rate singers! No, a
singer can't be created through training. Every throat,
each set of vocal chords, is different; every talent is special.

And every singer uses a distinct intellectual process when singing.

I want to emphasize that in his own uncanny way Maestro Ruax had an infallible instinct when it came to how I worked. He knew when to criticize without running the risk of stifling that which was pouring out of me, my natural ability. He had an inspiring ground rule: "Follow your heart." "Do what your intuition tells you to do," he would say. "Never sacrifice a single accent, or note, or expression for the sake of technique."

Ruax was the complete opposite of those unbending, overbearing singing teachers who from time immemorial have forced a certain method on their students. It hurts me to think of how many young singers have ruined their voices trying to follow rules that were not meant for them.

Singing lessons with Ruax were enjoyable. During a typical session, we would just sit and talk about singing for about an hour and a half; then he set aside about thirty minutes for actually practicing. But in all those wonderful afternoons I spent with him, I don't think I ever sang for more than twenty minutes at a time. He saw no purpose in forcing me to practice one scale after another, although ninety percent of the music teachers of the world punish their students this way.

In addition to talking about music, Ruax had another unique and pleasant teaching method. For hours, we'd listen to records, analyzing the tenor part. The Maestro believed it was important to know how each tenor, past and present, sang a certain piece of music. He wanted me to notice and learn how a particular tenor approached a whole work or how he made his way through a specific aria. He felt that a singer should become familiar with as many singing techniques and styles as possible—including those used by the greatest tenors. He claimed that only after understanding and mastering what others have already done could I hope to create my own way.

For me, this method clicked. I always had a natural instinct for music, so it suited me to search for my own style. Nor was it difficult for me to master the learning process that supported it. I had a different problem, one uniquely my own. To have my voice always ready, to make it flow at the drop of a hat—was, and still is, a challenge for me. I envy those colleagues of mine who can jump out of bed at six o'clock in the morning and belt out a high "C" before their first cup of coffee! Sounds like a fantasy, but it's true!

In the end, it was Ruax who changed the way I think about opera. Before I studied with him, I didn't think too much about the libretto. The story-line of an opera seemed superfluous. As far as I was concerned, the music—and only the music—had relevance and value. But this isn't true. Ruax helped me to see that a singer must immerse himself as completely as possible in his role: he must feel what the character is feeling. I learned then that we must be fully aware of our own feelings if we are to communicate feelings to others. Specific emotions and states of mind are expressed through music—the melody—but they're not random happenings: they're defined exactly by the librettist, and his text determines the choices in a composer's musical "language." To speak this language well, a singer must understand life—because that's what he is singing about. It was Ruax, himself immobilized by life, who taught me that we must live life fully, that we must savour intensely each moment, each second, making the most of each opportunity to the end. Only then can we express each modulation and colour, each musical phrase with its true meaning and proper value.

My teacher was well versed in these truths, and he imparted them to me, knowing instinctively and consciously where my strengths lay, knowing that I could never be a singer who relies only on technique. He was so right. Throughout my career I've always tried my best to follow his ideals.

The fact that I prefer interpretation over technique probably explains my taste when it comes to tenors. After my lessons with Ruax, I'd go home and head straight for my record collection. No matter who I started with, I always ended up with Giuseppe Di Stefano. Sometimes I'd listen to Enrico Caruso, Beniamino Gigli, Jussi Bjoerling, Richard Tucker, and Franco Corelli, all magnificent tenors. Their recordings were like voice lessons. But when I really wanted to *enjoy* myself, I took one of Pippo's records from the shelf. To listen to Di Stefano is to be enveloped in emotions pouring out with the voice through the music.

The first time I saw Di Stefano, in 1962 on the stage of the Liceo, he was singing Riccardo in *Un ballo in maschera.* More than any other tenor, he impressed me with the simple truth that singing is a pleasure. For me this was a confirmation of everything I believed in because I, too, love to sing. I admire many tenors and have been inspired by many of them, but only Di Stefano touched my soul. His own place in opera history is assured since he changed so many things in the art of Italian opera. Once only sound was important, and the definition of "sound" included the beauty and timbre of the voice. Since Di Stefano, however, the public, and especially the Italians, want to understand and feel every word in the score as well.

Through the years, I've performed in all the important opera houses of the world, but I never lost contact with my teacher. During the summer of 1987, I telephoned him several times—not from the theatre, but from the Hospital Clinico in Barcelona. A sad twist of fate brought us together again; by the fall of 1987, my octogenarian friend was himself admitted to the same hospital.

Unfortunately, I was quarantined in a sterile, barren room of the hematology unit undergoing the third phase of my chemotherapy. Though Ruax was just two floors above, we couldn't visit. One day in October, Juan Ruax died. I wanted to leave the hospital to attend his funeral, but the doctors wouldn't hear of it, so I was not able to extend this last courtesy to my friend and teacher.

I'll always remember Ruax. I know he was very proud of me, for he thought of me as more than his student. In a way, he looked on me as his artistic son. And he was the typical artistic father because whenever I found a moment to visit him at his home in Barcelona, he always managed to criticize me more than praise me. But his criticism was always softened by his own unique sense of humour. There is one anecdote that illustrates the special way he had with me. From time to time, I'd call the Maestro from some corner of the world.

"Maestro," I'd complain, "I don't know what's happening. Something's wrong with my high 'C'." And Ruax would answer, "I don't know why you're so upset, José. You never *had* a high 'C'."

12

First Successes
in Spain and Italy

I KNOW exactly when I made my life's decision. The time came at the close of the 1967-1968 academic year, and the question really had two parts to it: should I continue with my studies and join the family business, or should I devote myself exclusively to a career in singing? A family council was called. We went through long discussions, looking at my options from every conceivable angle, and finally we decided on a career in opera. I have to be honest, I never would have chosen a life in chemistry!

And so, the course was set. By a strange coincidence, I had my first television appearance in the fall of 1968. One day a friend of mine who worked at the Hotel Manila in Barcelona informed me that the important music critic Antonio Fernandez Cid had just checked in for a brief stay. At that time, Cid had his own television show, and many young artists were first seen on his program, after which they'd go on to build successful careers. My friend convinced me that all I had to do was to simply walk into the Hotel and sing something for Mr. Cid! Believe it or not, I did.

Cid listened to several of my songs and arias and was visibly moved. He particularly liked my rendition of

"Amor ti vieta" from *Fedora* and invited me to repeat it on his show. Of course, I accepted. It was an exciting offer, and I was proud to be part of his program. In his opening remarks, Mr. Cid predicted a bright future for me, which was quite a booster for my young career.

But soon my future acquired a more definite direction. A few months after my television stint, to be precise, during the 1969 Easter season, my singing coach Juan Ruax deemed that I was ready to take on something bigger and better, and he urged me to try out for the Gran Teatro del Liceo, which, at the time, remained under the direction of Juan Antonio Pamias. I felt very daring. At the audition I sang an aria from *La traviata* and then followed it by one from *Carmen*. When I finished, Pamias and his assistant went into a huddle out of earshot; after a moment of discussion in low voices, Pamias turned and informed me that the opera company was preparing a spectacular event for the upcoming season: a brand new production of Bellini's *Norma*, in which the incomparable Montserrat Caballé would sing the title role for the first time in her life. This important role debut would be accompanied by such names as Mario del Monaco and Fiorenza Cossotto. And then Pamias offered me a part in this glittering production: Flavio. "Look at the score and tell me in a week if you think you can do it," he said.

Who needed a week? The second his words were out, I had decided to accept! Although the role of Flavio is only a walk-on with a few phrases, it was a fabulous chance for a beginner to share the stage with these great names of opera—and, naturally, a golden opportunity to become known. But this was not all. As if in passing, Pamias dropped another bomb on me. They were also planning a new production of Verdi's *Nabucco*, and they needed a tenor. He believed I was ready to tackle it. I accepted his offer to appear in *Norma* and signed my very first contract, which gave me an enormous salary, enough to pay for the subway between my home and the opera house.

The premiere of *Norma* took place in January of 1970 and was a huge success for its stars even though Del Monaco bowed out at the last moment, being replaced by Bruno Prevedi. The critics noticed me in my tiny role and wrote about me, along with the others. They praised my voice and predicted a future on the stage for me.

So I was "in," the ice was broken. But this production of *Norma* would prove to be more than a successful performance for me. It also marked the beginning of one of the deepest friendships of my life—my very special relationship with Montserrat Caballé. I already knew her brother, Carlos, who was her manager and whom I met when I was studying with Maestro Puig. Carlos had once visited my teacher in order to contact one of Puig's soprano students, and had walked in on one of my lessons. After hearing me sing, he told me, "The day you think you're finished with your training, let me know. We may be able to do something together." And this was it. Not only a houseful of opera goers had heard me; I was also heard by Montserrat Caballé, Carlos's sister. The great diva was so pleased by my voice and by my style of delivery that she wished me to partner her in the forthcoming production. But this time I would be a principal!

I knew it meant the beginning of my career. Naturally, there was some envy backstage; it was rumoured about that it wasn't difficult to make one's debut at the Liceo as long as one was sponsored by the great Montserrat Caballé. I didn't care about such talk because I believed that the best connection in the world couldn't help me if I didn't have the ability to match. On the other hand, one failure would very probably kill my career before it began.

I will always remember how much Montserrat Caballé trusted in my talent and competence. The mere fact that a soprano of her calibre had expressed a desire to sing with a newcomer was such news that everybody focused on me even before the opening night. This was quite an advantage, professionally speaking. But what really meant the world to me was her moral support. You can't imagine how buoyed I felt because a great artist like La Caballé believed in me, a beginner. It was her help that made me strong.

So after *Norma* in January, I was given my first leading role, Gennaro, in Donizetti's *Lucrezia Borgia*, which we performed that very same year. The opera tells a rather convoluted story of mistaken identity; the tenor falls in love with Lucrezia, unaware that she's his mother. The best review I received about my performance that evening was by Montserrat herself. Years later, in a television interview, she laughingly recalled the premiere and said, "As a mother, one couldn't wish for a better son!"

Speaking of "mother" and "son", for years I've been asked how singers manage love scenes when they're obviously mismatched. I'd come across as a very young man while Montserrat, judged superficially, possesses a more mature air. Let me tell you that I have appeared with her more than two hundred times, and each time she has put me under her spell. I'm a lost man when I sing with her; I fall in love right there on the stage. Of all the prima donnas I know, she more than anyone becomes the person she is portraying. She's simply incredible. A perfect example of this was her performance in Cilea's *Adriana Lecouvreur*, produced in September 1976 in Tokyo. Never before or since has a soprano sung with me as beautifully in character as Montserrat.

In any case, I look back on the Barcelona premiere of *Lucrezia Borgia* in December of 1970 as my debut. The two child roles and my appearance as Flavio had been rather like a preliminary rehearsal.

After *Lucrezia Borgia* I was given the tenor role in the new production of *Nabucco*, just as Director Pamias had said, and although I didn't realize it at the time the stage for my next big adventure was being set.

It was Giuseppe Tomasi, our stage director and a great connoisseur of voices, who was the inspiration for the next decisive step in my career: he urged me fervently to participate in the celebrated Verdi Singing Competition in Parma. "Believe me," he said, "you have a good chance of winning, and if it doesn't work out, at least it'll give you more experience. Besides, an appearance in Parma would be your introduction to Italy."

I wasn't very confident about this idea because my first and last competition held in Barcelona in 1968 hadn't brought me any recognition at all. But both Tomasi and Carlos Caballé kept insisting that I should try my luck at Parma, and finally I agreed to go. What helped my decision was the knowledge that the Parma competition is one of the most prestigious in the world. It was apparent to me that many of my colleagues had successfully used this famous contest as a springboard for their careers. Besides, there were two more immediate advantages, the prize money and an engagement at the Parma opera house.

For the preliminary round in July of 1971, I sang Rodolfo's aria from Verdi's *Luisa Miller*, following it with the "Flower Song" from *Carmen* since we were allowed to sing arias by other composers even though it was a Verdi event. I soon found out there was no need to be afraid of the audience; the people of Parma are very generous, particularly, to young singers. But when something doesn't work, they show their displeasure much more vehemently than audiences do elsewhere. It isn't so much a badly hit note or even a completely lost one that causes the fans to scold the singer; what they can't abide is an unconvincing interpretation, bad style, or lack of musicality.

Well, my singing pleased the judges enough so that I could make it to the finals, which were held the following October. And it was with Riccardo's romanza from the last act of *Un ballo in maschera* that I finally managed to snatch victory in this famous contest!

The exciting experience in Parma will forever be linked in my mind with an event that I had dreamed about for many years. It was there that I met my idol and role-model, Giuseppe Di Stefano. Much later I heard the story of how Di Stefano was urged by someone to attend without fail the Parma contest that year since there was going to be a young Spaniard who sang exactly like Di Stefano had in his youth.

I remember the respect and awe with which we, the young contestants, waited for Di Stefano. The great tenor arrived in his Rolls Royce and proceeded to greet us courteously, exchanging a few kind words with each one of us. Just like the rest of our group, I was terribly excited, and when I saw the great Pippo in front of me I began shaking like jelly. But the high point of his visit came later when he attended the finals, following the action from a box near the stage. From the corner of my eye, I could see his face and watch his expressions. After I was named the winner, Di Stefano came backstage to congratulate me. He expressed confidence in my new career and then asked me, as if it were an afterthought, "Have you, by any chance, ever listened to a record of mine?" It was all I could do not to burst out laughing.

My Parma adventure wasn't over until I faced the "ordeal by fire": singing in performance before the fabled opera audience of that city. This was the ultimate test, one that would hopefully garner me the approval of the people. As the competition winner, I was promised the part of Rodolfo in two performances of *La Bohème*. I was partnered by the previous year's winner, Katia Ricciarelli, as Mimi. The performances were such a runaway success that I was invited to sing in the next year's season opener, *Un ballo in maschera*.

Yes, I remember *that* episode very well. Even before we opened there had been a storm of controversy brewing. The public thought there were far too many foreigners in the *Ballo* cast: my Amelia was to be the then totally unknown Ghena Dimitrova, and the only Italian in any significant role was Piero Cappuccilli. Although the unions in particular objected to this state of affairs, loud protests were also heard from the regulars in the auditorium. They let it be emphatically known that there were at least ten Italian tenors who could sing Riccardo and that there was certainly no need to bring a Spaniard to Parma! Because of all the uproar, the performance was late in starting, but it was allowed to proceed. After the last notes of my opening aria—the first great aria of the opera—faded away, applause broke through the house. I heard shouts of "Bravo! Bravo!" and I knew then that I had this fateful evening in the palm of my hand.

After Europe, America: from New York to California. Here, in *La Bohème*, San Francisco, 1973.

13

New York, Vienna, Milan

I SEE no point in recounting chronologi-
cally the various stages of my career and going over each
place and appearance in minute detail. I'd like to paint a
broader picture of the events, drawing attention only to
those that I consider personally or professionally memorable.

After my debut in Barcelona, things had settled down
into a routine. As expected, I'd made the rounds of various
opera houses. In 1971, I performed mostly in Barcelona, although I did appear in Minorca, Teneriffe, and finally
Madrid. My most unusual performance at that time was my
debut in the leading role of Alfredo in Verdi's *La traviata*.
This performance stands out in my mind because it was in
Prague, my first appearance behind the Iron Curtain.

From 1971 through 1973, I made my debut in many opera houses around the world, sometimes in concert versions that included *Maria Stuarda, I Lombardi, Lucia di Lammermoor, Rigoletto, La Bohème, Luisa Miller, Don Carlos,
Madama Butterfly, Mefistofele, Adriana Lecouvreur, L'elisir
d'amore, Catarina Cornaro*, and *Tosca*. Of these, I found
Donizetti's *Catarina Cornaro* at the London Royal Festival
Hall to be the most exciting. Giacomo Aragall had been

scheduled to sing the tenor role, but he fell ill and had to cancel. What a surprise when they called me to ask if I'd be interested in taking over. Of course, I was interested! But there was one catch: I didn't know the opera, much less the tenor role. I accepted anyway; it was a challenge I couldn't resist! I buried myself in the score, and thirty-six hours later, there I stood on the Festival Hall stage—a brand new Geraldo—with the famed Montserrat Caballé singing Catarina. The marathon hours of preparation paid off; despite my battle of nerves, things turned out remarkably well.

In the early years of my career while I was acquiring experience in several cities abroad, the most important foreign contract that I signed was with the City Opera in New York. Being associated with this company greatly extended my theatrical and musical horizons. In some aspects, I was still a greenhorn, and my colleagues and the management there were very helpful to me. It's better for a young singer to earn his beginner's wages in a renowned opera house than in some obscure provincial theatre. With the New York's City Opera, I had the chance to sing in quality productions and to work with a distinguished orchestra. It was also during this time that I began to fathom what each composer expected from a singer when he wrote the music; it was in New York that my taste acquired a specific direction and I uncovered my own interpretive style.

New York holds the key to opera in America and, in fact, to the whole world. If one can make it in New York, every other operatic mountain is but a foothill. It didn't matter that I hadn't yet appeared in the legendary Metropolitan Opera; for a young singer like me, the smaller and less known City Opera was a formidable enough starting point. Just a mention in *The New York Times* is a dream come true for a new singer, and for me it was already a reality! The best part of being with the City Opera, however, was that I learned what it means to work in repertory. I had the chance for the first time in my life to sing roles such as Pinkerton and Cavaradossi. The management even allowed me to sing opposite the legendary Birgit Nilsson in *Tosca* during a tour. I remember this great leading lady referring to me as "My baby Cavaradossi"!

Once I had New York stage credits, my career took a fantastic upswing. Almost overnight I had many offers, and I was in the unaccustomed but comfortable position of being able to choose the most attractive. A few months after my twenty-seventh birthday I appeared in most of the famous opera houses in the world, one after another, with dizzying speed.

My first house debut in this prestigious series was at the Vienna Staatsoper in January 1974. Sad to say, I had everything going for me that evening but luck. I was cast as the Duke in *Rigoletto*, a role that I have loved since childhood, but when I reached the dramatic point at the end of "La donna e mobile", an aria I had sung a thousand times if I had sung it once, my voice gave out. Something like this happens to a singer perhaps once in ten years. How horrifying that it had to happen to me so early in my career and in Vienna, the City of Music! The feared Viennese audience remained stoically silent; I don't remember hearing one cat call from the standing room. In the end, they even applauded me in a rather friendly way.

On the whole, that evening in Vienna was nothing to write home about, and I'd rather forget it, but my manager, Carlos Caballé, will probably never let me. Later, whenever I had to decline a lucrative offer because of a previous commitment, Carlos would quip, "Just sing your Duke from *Rigoletto*, and they'll let you out of that contract!" He still likes to use this line on me. Nevertheless, in the end, and for several reasons, Vienna was to become my second home. But for a few years, while the embarrassment was fresh, I kept a healthy distance.

In March 1974, I made my debuts in two other important European opera houses. First, I made a guest appearance as Alfredo in *La traviata* at London's Royal Opera House. Then I played Cavaradossi, substituting for Franco Corelli, at the Munich National Theatre. Several months later I returned to New York, this time to the Metropolitan Opera itself. At the Met, I performed the role of Cavaradossi again, appearing with Rachel Mathes and the enthralling Robert Merrill.

In just ten short months, I had done so much: Vienna, London, Munich, New York. In February 1975, when I was engaged to sing in Milan, I felt I had reached the pinnacle. To perform at La Scala is every opera singer's dream. I consider my first appearance in the most famous opera theatre of the world to be a major milestone in my career. What was even more fantastic, I was offered my favourite role, that of Riccardo in Verdi's *Un ballo in maschera*. Maestro Francesco Molinari-Pradelli was scheduled to conduct, Montserrat Caballé was Amelia, and Renato Bruson was to be Renato.

As soon as I arrived in Milan, I was delighted to once again get together with Giuseppe Di Stefano. Pippo invited me to dine with him at his elegant apartment near La Scala. I discovered Di Stefano was not only a great opera singer but also an extraordinary man. He had a unique personality, known to be uncommonly obliging to everyone, and he had a delightful sense of humour. He also had the compassion and capacity to listen to the worries and fears of younger colleagues, such as the likes of me.

Tenors, by and large, are not very interesting conversationalists; they usually only want to talk about two things: their voice or their career. But Pippo had, and still has, a knack for steering discussions in a direction that had nothing at all to do with opera or singing. He is a born storyteller, with hundreds of interesting, educational, or funny stories in his pocket. Of course, some were opera anecdotes but I had the feeling he especially loved to bring up his own funny blunders and goof-ups on the stage. He would joke about those times when he really "blew it" and knocked his image of hero down a peg or two.

I was lucky that Di Stefano and I met when we did, for our getting together for dinner that evening was to have a memorable consequence on my forthcoming house debut in *Ballo*.

Pippo showed up unexpectedly at the opera house to watch our dress rehearsal. With his professional eye, he quietly observed the first act. Then, during the break, he burst into my dressing room and objected excitedly: "Listen here, José! You can't make your debut at La Scala in that costume! It doesn't fit you, and besides it's dreadful! It won't do!"

He was right, I was swimming in that old costume. The Riccardo for whom it had been made was a more robust, heavier-set tenor; even though La Scala employs first-rate tailors, they declared it difficult to trim this enormous raiment to fit my figure.

When the rehearsal was over, Di Stefano whisked me off to his apartment. When we got there he showed me his private costume collection. It was unbelievable. Pippo had absolutely hundreds of costumes stored inside wardrobe crates. He rummaged through all kinds of outfits for some time, finally pulling out triumphantly what he'd been looking for. He announced with satisfaction, "This is the costume I wore when I sang my first Riccardo at La Scala." The debut he was referring to was the now legendary production in which he had appeared with Maria Callas, Giulietta Simionato, and Ettore Bastianini. Then he added, "Now you will sing in it."

And that is what happened. I appeared on stage wearing Pippo's famous costume. I can't tell you how proud I was of this gift, and to this day it has a place of honour in my home. Need I say that on opening night at La Scala that costume did wonders for my confidence?

In the theatre business, secrets don't stay secrets for long, so the word soon got around that the great Pippo had given the young Carreras his *Ballo* costume. Milan's opera fans started looking forward to the opening even more, waiting anxiously to get a glimpse of me. Milan audiences have the reputation of being mercilessly critical when it comes to a role that is regarded as the domain of Italian tenors. Yet they enthusiastically accepted me, a Spaniard. My Scala debut on February 13, 1975, turned out to be a huge success—my greatest triumph to date. As soon as I had sung my first aria, I knew that I had the audience in my hand, and I felt that indescribable sensation that you get as a performer when you know that your delivery is going to be flawless. At times like this, you literally drink in the music. You feel in total control of your role. And the give-and-take between you and your partner is just as planned. There are no surprises. Everything is exactly perfect.

After my cabaletta before the last scene, I heard spontaneous shouts from the audience; the outbursts were loud enough to drown out the music for several seconds. I experienced a fantastic moment, when even a veteran performer would get goose flesh.

The next morning I received dazzling reviews. And, in

the end, it was because of this La Scala performance that my name was brought to the attention of one of the all-time greats in the world of music, Herbert von Karajan.

Overleaf.
A symbolic picture: arm upraised, Herbert von Karajan, the guiding spirit of my artistic life, directs me as Radames, in the rehearsal of *Aida*, Salzburg 1979. My voice was an elemental material with which he formed his operatic structures.

14

Working with Herbert von Karajan

O<small>NLY MUCH</small> later did I discover how my name had been brought to the attention of Herbert von Karajan. Andre von Mattoni, Karajan's closest confidant (since deceased), and Peter Busse, the Maestro's long-time assistant, were in the audience for my debut in *Un Ballo in maschera* at La Scala. Both men reported to Karajan about a young Spanish tenor he should take the time to audition. Life being what it is, nothing happened immediately. But a few months later, Emil Jucker, Karajan's manager at the time, asked Carlos Caballé, my manager, if I'd be available during April 1976. Maestro Karajan wished to engage me for Verdi's *Requiem Mass* during the Easter Festival in Salzburg.

What an offer! By this time I had already appeared in most of the famous opera houses in the world, but I hadn't yet made it to Salzburg. To perform there at Easter time or in any of the Salzburg summer festival productions is a high point in the career of any singer. The world's most renowned orchestras and the leading conductors and soloists perform there during the season. Money is no object for the festival organizers, and the opera productions are first-rate regardless of whether they please all tastes. Someone once told me that you can be booked to sing in small provincial theatres for most of the year, but as long as you have had at least one summer engagement in Salzburg, you're on your way up and your career is going places. The flip side of the coin is that you could have performed in a large opera house throughout a whole year, but if you don't make it to Salzburg, you're still considered a provincial singer. Salzburg makes the difference. To top it all, if you were lucky enough to be in a production directed by the esteemed Karajan, it would mean an even greater honour, and the prestige would certainly give you an enormous standing.

Although I was familiar with most of Karajan's recordings, I had never actually watched him conduct in person either in an opera house or in a concert hall. At most, I may have seen him in a performance on television. He once conducted the Berlin Philharmonic Orchestra in Barcelona at the Music Palace, but I had missed him because I was not in town at the time.

Things were not meant to change even now. Fate had it that I wouldn't set my eyes on Karajan until our first rehearsal for the *Requiem*. In my case, the Maestro had waived the usual preliminary audition and, while this pleased me, I was all the more nervous about meeting him.

I will never forget our first encounter. A day before we started work on the *Requiem* he telephoned me at my hotel to go over several details in the score and let me know what he had in mind. He bade me good-bye with a curt, "I'll see you at the rehearsal tomorrow, at eleven."

Eleven in the morning! This was a terrible hour for me since it didn't fit my sleep pattern at all. A workday for opera singers is mostly in the evening, and typically some performances don't end until well after midnight, especially in the southern countries. It's completely impossible to go to sleep right after a performance. No matter how exhausted my body can be, my head is wide awake—I need some time to wind down and to work my way through the evening's presentation, emotionally and mentally. For this reason I've become accustomed to going to bed very late and sleeping away most of the next morning. Usually I wake up on my own, as my body lets me know when it has had enough rest. But there are times, unfortunately, when my regular sleep cycle is disturbed either because of an early flight or because of conferences and various appointments which break my routine. And rehearsals are definitely unavoidable. But for me a rehearsal with Herbert von Karajan was not just any run through! I decided that I'd prepare for this rehearsal just as seriously as I would prepare for a premiere in a famous opera house.

I got up hours before the appointed time, to be exact, at six in the morning, and started warming up my voice. I was simply tortured by the specter of not being in form. "Let the voice flow freely," I kept ordering myself. "Otherwise he'll kick you out at once!"

By the time I marched out on the stage of the great Salzburg festival house with the other soloists — Montserrat Caballé, Fiorenza Cossotto, and José van Dam — I was feeling rotten. I hadn't felt that sick in a long time.

Karajan arrived in a very good mood. He had a friendly word for everyone, and when someone introduced us he greeted me briefly. Then we went right to work.

I think if this had been an opera rehearsal, things would have gone better for me. The conductor would have been a safe distance away, the space of the whole orchestra pit between us. But in a Mass you find yourself directly in front of him; I stood just three feet away from the Maestro.

This was much too close for comfort, my comfort, at any rate! To make matters worse, in Verdi's *Requiem*, the tenor is the first to sing.

Then it happened! The most dreadful thing imaginable: I opened my mouth to sing Kyrie Eleison, but nothing came out. I couldn't produce a single note, not then, and not later. During the whole rehearsal, the only thing I could do was mark time.

"That's it. I'm through," I told myself, although Karajan didn't so much as blink an eye to show what he thought about his new tenor. I was fully aware how important this rehearsal was for my future as I had already been informed, earlier, that Karajan was probably going to give me the role of Don Carlos the following summer. All during my voiceless *Requiem* rehearsal I felt I could kiss that project good-bye.

After the rehearsal, the Maestro said a few encouraging words to me, but nothing that would substantially change my deep dejection. I didn't even dare ask what would happen to me now. It was only later that I heard about my immediate future in Salzburg. A woman from the costume department called. She wanted to take my measurements for the Don Carlos costume.

The Verdi *Requiem* on April 10, 1976, was a huge success and the beginning of my wonderful years of collaboration with Maestro Herbert von Karajan. I have no doubts whatsoever that this was the most extraordinary and important relationship in my artistic life. The fact that at the beginning of our work together I was still relatively "undeveloped" as an artist meant a lot to the Maestro. His offer to sing for him came rather early in my career, and I was, so to speak, virgin clay for him to form operatically. Karajan saw the chance to mold a young singer, and I'm sure the thought appealed to him. My voice was something he had always dreamt about: the elemental material with which he could build.

It was fascinating how Karajan made you feel that he was like your father, conducting for you alone. There you were on the stage, under the impression that you were calling all the shots and that he would always follow you with the orchestra. It was all an illusion because in reality everything was turned around. He did it in such a way that you wouldn't notice it. Here was one of the great professional secrets of Karajan's art of conducting. You thought you were singing as freely as you pleased and your confidence soared; yet all the time he was leading you from the beginning through to the end of the work. Mirella Freni once put it this way: "Singing with Karajan was like going to sleep in a comfortable bed."

Many spectators and most critics preferred Karajan the conductor to Karajan the stage director. You would read or hear that the Maestro's staging was "old fashioned" and "conventional." This criticism may have been true, but I judge the Maestro differently. Karajan was a man of the theatre: he understood that there must be a co-operative relationship and consistency between the action on the stage and the music. He was also a consummate musician; he knew what his singers could do and, conversely, what they couldn't or shouldn't do. To my knowledge, be never asked a singer to behave on the stage in a way that would go against the music. For us singers such artistic policy is much more important—in fact, essential—than the most original ideas of an eccentric stage director. Karajan believed as I do: "When in doubt, follow the music."

It's true that Karajan had the reputation of being a very difficult man. He was often described as "inaccessible" and "distant" in his attitude towards others, "domineering" or "dictatorial" at work. Some of my colleagues, I must admit, had problems with him and at times even fierce quarrels. Speaking for myself, we never had the smallest disagreement. I can't recall his ever making a sarcastic remark if I made a mistake, nor was I ever maliciously criticized or condemned even at times when I didn't quite live up to his expectations.

Karajan treated me with affectionate concern. In May, 1987, I was in Austria taking part in a gala concert, my leg in a cast due to a minor tennis injury. Karajan saw the programme on television and, being concerned, called me the following day to ask what had happened. Later, when I was hospitalized for so long in Barcelona and in Seattle, he contacted me repeatedly, to encourage me and tell me I was included in his future plans.

I never felt the Maestro to be unapproachable or distant, quite the opposite. In fact, I often had the pleasure of talking with him about things that had nothing to do with music. Besides, he could be outrageously witty, which meant that he could take joking from others. I remember a story which showed his sense of humour. He once had some business with me and told me when to meet him. "I'm sorry, Maestro," I answered, "I can't make it that day; I have a concert in Oviedo."

"And what the devil is 'Oviedo'?" Karajan asked in mock horror.

Knowing that the German town of Ulm figured early in his career, I answered: "Well, Maestro, it's something like Ulm." Karajan had a good laugh, but there were some people around him who thought my teasing was an insult to the great man.

Another time when someone got the wrong impression about Karajan was in 1978, in Salzburg, where we were again performing Verdi's *Requiem*. This time I sang with Mirella Freni, Agnes Baltsa, and Nicolai Ghiaurov. A

Here I am, on July 21, 1988, under the Arch of Triumph in Barcelona: my greatest wish is being fulfilled.

Queen Sofia hon-
ored me with her
presence at my
second Spanish
concert after my
illness.

July 21, 1988 was
also a great thrill for
my daughter Julia:
she offered flowers
to the Queen
(above).
The Princess of
Wales, Queen Ana
Maria of Greece and
Princess Irene
attended my recital
in Peralada the fol-
lowing month,
August 13, 1988.

October 1988:
I took part in a
benefit concert in
Paris. Afterward,
I was visited by
Queen Noor Al
Hussein of Jordan
and, of course, by
Julia.

September 16, 1988: unforgettable day when, after a long absence, I sang again on the stage of an opera house. The recital in the legendary Vienna Staatsoper lasted three hours, one more than scheduled. I'll always remember it.

In spite of the night chill, five thousand people gathered in the square of the Staatsoper to watch the concert on a gigantic screen.

Another milestone in my life took place on December 10, 1988: I gave
a concert in the Sala Nervi of the Vatican. Pope John II could not attend,
but he saw me in a private audience.

Here I am, in short pants, before our Argentina adventure. At the time I had no inkling of my desire to sing—but that fateful moment was at hand . . .

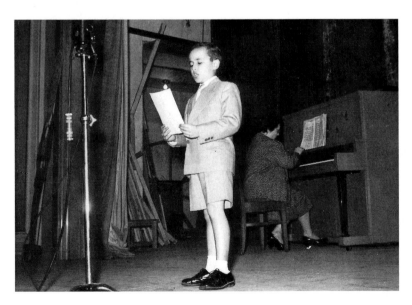

My first public appearance! I was eight when the Spanish National Radio invited me to join a benefit program for needy children. I sang a Catalan Christmas carol and, of course, "La donna e mobile."

It was fun to be a conductor or a pianist. After my debut in *El Retablo del Maese Pedro* at the Liceo I proudly posed with our Don Quixote, the famous Manuel Ausensi.

My family felt great pride when I appeared for the first time in the famous Liceo of Barcelona.

Here we are at the gala banquet after my opening night. My parents didn't even dream that singing would be my life.

Barcelona, 1970: As Gennaro in Donizetti's *Lucrecia Borgia,* I was partnering the great Montserrat Caballé for the second time—my first principal role.

Parma, 1972: my first Rodolfo in *La Bohème.* The performance took place after I won the Verdi Competition.

Barcelona, 1970. During this eventful year I had my adult house debut at the Liceo as Flavio in Bellini's *Norma*, and a little later I sang my first principal role there: as Ismael in Verdi's *Nabucco*.

With Alberto and Julia in our garden. Our oldest friend and pet, the german shepherd Lido, had to be in this picture.

In 1985 I filmed a holiday television program in the famous *Stille Nacht* chapel in Oberndorf near Salzburg. Alberto and Julia came to see me at work.

A memory from Verona: Alberto came to see me during the run of *Andrea Chenier* in the Arena, summer of 1986.

I was always sorry that there was so little time for friendly football games like this one in the woods near Vienna.

Top, on tour with the
New York City
Opera *Tosca*, Los
Angeles, 1974. I had
the privilege of part-
nering Birgit Nilsson,
who called me her
"Baby Cavaradossi."
Left, as Rodolfo in *La
Bohème*, Covent
Garden, London,
1976. Puccini's poet
is one of my
favourite roles.

As Pinkerton in *Madama Butterfly*, in Covent Garden, London. I first sang this role in 1972 for the New York City Opera.

Nemorino is one of my favourite roles. Sir Geraint Evans and I shared the stage in this scene of *L'elisir d'amore* at Covent Garden, London.

With Montserrat Caballé: in 1977 as Roberto, during a performance of Donizetti's *Roberto Devereux*, at the Aix-en-Provence festival. Left: in 1979 during a rehearsal for *Tosca*, at the Vienna Staatsoper.

In the title role of *Andrea Chenier* in Vienna, 1986.

D. José in *Carmen*, at the Met, 1987.

Here is a moment that can't be staged in any production of *Carmen!* A snapshot with my very special colleague Agnes - backstage, naturally.

friend of mine who saw the performance mentioned later that the four of us looked rather comical taking our bows next to our Maestro, like students who were afraid of their teacher. He said that he could feel an invisible wall between us and Karajan.

His impression was totally wrong. What may have seemed a barrier was in reality a distance imposed by respect and admiration for the man whom we considered a great conductor, so great that to us he was like a supernatural being. Karajan made music like no one else in the world. For him everything could be built and revealed with logic. As the result of this unparalleled logic, the music he created always had tremendous depth.

In addition to everything else about him, I was consistently impressed by Karajan's iron-clad self-discipline. He was always the first to arrive and last to leave, and in all the years I knew him he was never a minute late for a rehearsal. It's understandable, then, that being this kind of a man, he demanded the same professionalism from others. He wouldn't tolerate a lack of discipline. And I always tried to work as hard as I could at his rehearsals, utilizing all my five senses in the creative process. That Karajan didn't always ask for such total commitment is another matter.

If he believed in you and trusted you, Karajan had a way of showing his feelings by going easy on you, protecting you. For example, sometimes I would sing with a full voice during rehearsals. He would imperceptibly gesture to me, letting me know that I should take it easier. It was as if he were saying, "Don't tire yourself out. When I need you, I'll let you know." This is how it would happen, that in a three hour rehearsal I'd end up singing with a full voice no more than a minute. Only someone who's had a similar experience with Karajan can understand how an artist feels about this show of confidence. I can't deny the fact that other conductors may be easier going, but the benefit of making music with a taskmaster like Karajan was that it revealed new aspects and unsuspected dimensions in the difficult art of opera. So much of what I have learned and what I have discovered with Karajan's guidance I could later use elsewhere throughout my career.

On the other hand, if you were lucky enough to have regular contracts with the Maestro, as I did, your reputation would naturally grow from your association with him. After a while, even those opera fans who never counted me among their favourite singers had to admit at some point, "If Karajan chooses to work with him so much, this Carreras must be somewhat special. At least he must be musical and have a professional attitude about singing."

Karajan involved me in great projects; from 1976 until his death, we steadily collaborated. First, the *Messa da Requiem* at the Salzburg Easter Festival. Then in the same summer, we did Verdi's *Don Carlos*. For the Easter seasons of 1977, 1978, and 1986, we again performed *Don Carlos*; in 1979 and 1980, we did this Verdi opera again in Vienna. I felt that our next planned project, *La Bohème* at the Vienna Staatsoper, would be the high point of my career.

It is well-known that it was in Milan, with their joint production of *La Bohème* at La Scala in the 1960's, that Karajan and Franco Zeffirelli made history. I read about it in the newspapers. Di Stefano had been promised the tenor role by the La Scala's directors, but Karajan, objecting to this decision, hired the young Gianni Raimondi. On opening night, the fans of both of these tenors started a shouting match in the theatre, the likes of which had never been heard before. Yet by the end of the evening, the opening was acclaimed as one of the greatest to ever take place at that illustrious theatre.

After a successful run at La Scala, the production

moved to the Vienna Staatsoper, where Karajan himself was the director; Mirella Freni and Gianni Raimondi continued in their roles. It was at the Staatsoper that *La Bohème* was filmed, and I couldn't begin to count the number of times I went to see that particular movie as a student. All of this had happened about fourteen years ago, and now Karajan wanted me to take the role of Rodolfo. He had been away from the Vienna State Opera for thirteen years, and his plan was that in May 1977 *La Bohème* would mark his return to the Staatsoper. This was when I realized for the first time how much opera means to the people of Vienna. With the exception of perhaps Milan, I don't think you'll find a city that's more enthusiastic about lyric drama.

Karajan gave Vienna a fantastic operatic schedule: *Il trovatore*, *La Bohème*, and *The marriage of Figaro*. Each of these he conducted three times, which added up to a memorable number of star-studded hours. People stood in line all night to buy tickets, even for standing room. Opera-goers in Vienna could talk of nothing else; there was an epidemic of Karajan fever.

For his comeback, Karajan opened with *Il trovatore*, with Luciano Pavarotti singing Manrico. Luciano and I had got to know each other in San Francisco two years before; we had spent a lot of time together. It goes without saying that Luciano is a sensational singer, but while we were in San Francisco, I learned that he's an even better poker player! Long nights of card-playing proved that. It was Giacomo Aragall who pulled our two teams together for a match: the *Luisa Miller* team with Luciano and Katia Ricciarelli and the *Butterfly* team with Renata Scotto and myself. One time Renata and I played a game that lasted the entire flight from Tokyo to Rome, and, by the time we reached Hong Kong for a stopover, she could buy a pearl ring with her winnings.

Before the Vienna opening, Luciano mentioned that I should try to get a close-up look at how the people in the audience react to Karajan. Well, that was easier said than done. The opening night tickets to *Il trovatore* were sold out, so Luciano offered me a ticket from his quota. That was how, surrounded by Italian-born Pavarotti fans and with a fantastic balcony view, I watched Vienna welcome back Karajan after his long absence.

When the Maestro stepped into the orchestra pit, the theatre reverberated with shrieks and commotion the likes of which I'd never heard before. The ovations lasted so long that I wondered if the performance was ever going to begin. Suddenly, almost brusquely, Karajan turned to face the orchestra. He directed one of the orchestra servants to remove a huge bouquet of red roses from the conductor's dais and then, amidst the roar, raised his arms. Instantly, a hush fell. The performance began.

Five days later, on May 13, 1977, I experienced this same ritual, only this time I wasn't in the balcony; I was on the stage. During the last few minutes before the curtain went up, my tension was indescribable, my heart pounding wildly. I think Mirella felt the same way even though she'd had a longer association with Karajan and knew more of what to expect. The next day a famous Viennese music critic started his review with a statement that was truer than I'm sure he realized: "Last night, two opera stars and their conductor had—and caused—heart palpitations!" The critic went on to write, "They gave us a Puccini evening of total beauty. It had everything . . . ."

I couldn't say whether there was ever another time or place, before or since that performance, that I sang Rodolfo better. What I can say for sure is that the atmosphere surrounding that performance was a rare experience—and

I doubt that it could have happened anywhere but in Vienna.

Our third and last performance of *La Bohème* also happened to be Karajan's last guest appearance in Vienna. When the curtain fell, the audience refused to let him go. The ovations lasted for at least forty-five minutes, which is longer than the first act of *La Bohème*. Even the Austrian President stayed in his box seat until the end. Finally, the metal fire curtain was let down, but the audience continued to applaud and succeeded in getting it raised again so that all the performers had to be called back from their dressing rooms to take more bows. It was absolutely fantastic! The next year, when we returned to sing *La Bohème* again, the marvellous Vienna audience also repeated its performance.

About this time, Karajan became involved in another project: *Aida* at the Salzburg Festival. He offered me the role of Radames. Word of this was hardly out when everyone started advising me not to accept his offer, that it was too early in my career to sing Radames, that I might hurt my voice, and so on. Believe me, it was a difficult decision. I knew singing Radames was risky, but with Karajan conducting I was willing to chance it. He went over the role with me and explained what he had in mind: he didn't want a strong-voiced, ostentatious Radames. Instead he saw him as a sensitive lover. I thought to myself, "If a tenor can sing the love duet in *Un ballo in maschera*, is there any reason why he couldn't cope with the Nile scene?" It's true that "Celeste Aida" is an extremely demanding aria, and, unfortunately, it comes right at the beginning of the opera. But it's a lyric aria, and, if you think about it, Radames has quite a few lyrical passages throughout the opera, especially in the last act. On the other hand, the trial scene has its drawbacks—a high *tessitura* and heavy orchestration—and these could certainly be dangerous.

I accepted.

Our first ensemble rehearsal was held in Karajan's home in Mauerbach, near Vienna, and three months before *Aida* opened at the Salzburg Festival we recorded it at a Vienna studio. Everything seemed to be going well, so well that I came away from the recording session feeling quite satisfied.

But what a difference between the recording studio and the stage! The closer that our opening night came, the greater my emotional burden. I was slowly being overwhelmed by nervous tension. Karajan always seemed to be somewhere near, and he'd calm me down. Even when I was alone within my own four walls, I could feel his presence, possibly because I was renting a house in Anif, near Salzburg, that used to belong to him.

Karajan had an uncanny way of understanding how people felt. I found this out on the day *Aida* finally opened: July 26, 1979. It was almost lunchtime, and I felt that I just couldn't stay cooped up in the house any longer. My tension was unbearable. I visualized the great festival playhouse. In a few hours the curtain would rise on the *Aida* that everyone was waiting for (or lying in wait for). There would be a huge audience, the international press, a live radio broadcast.

To get my mind off these things, I went for a walk in the woods where I knew I'd be alone and no one could reach me. The ridiculous incident that followed shows how distraught I was. I was walking along a narrow path when I suddenly saw two men on motorcycles heading toward me. It was the police. "Here's the answer to my problem," I said to myself. "They've come to arrest me! Maybe for murder, or who knows what the hell for?" And I could bow out of *Aida*. It cheered me up to imagine the headlines: KARAJAN'S RADAMES JAILED IN SALZBURG! I played out the whole story in my mind quite successfully, but in a few seconds, the weird daydream ended. The two policemen sped right by. Arrest me? They hadn't even noticed me.

I wasn't in a much better state of mind when, about an hour later, I got back to the house. Things continued this way until the phone rang. It was Karajan. He told me he could imagine how I felt and that he knew such situations only too well, but all I had to do was to rely on him. We talked for a few minutes, long enough for me to calm down and get my courage back. Karajan was able to "heal" me and give me peace of mind just with one phone call. My fear of this debut almost disappeared, and to this day I'm grateful to the Maestro for that.

Aida was performed in Salzburg for two consecutive summers. I should mention that we played to a house that was always overbooked, something that hadn't happened in years. In fact, it was rumoured that six times as many tickets could have been sold.

In 1981 Karajan and I had a hiatus, only one concert of songs in Salzburg. In 1982 we gave a concert performance of *Tosca* in West Berlin, a concert that we had already commercially recorded, followed by several performances of Verdi's *Requiem* in various theatres. In 1985 we opened *Carmen*, with Agnes Baltsa, at the Easter Festival. That production carried over into the summer festival, as well as into the 1986 programme.

We had already recorded *Carmen* by that time in the fall of 1982. When we finished the session, Karajan said to me, "I'm seventy-four years old, and finally I hear someone sing the role of Don José the way I always dreamed it should be sung." This was, by far, the greatest compliment I'd ever been given—especially when you consider that Karajan seldom praised anyone.

In the summer of 1988, a few months after Karajan's eightieth birthday, I was passing through Salzburg and stopped to visit him. It was an emotional reunion; I had been away and ill for many months.

Now, Karajan is the one who is gone. My memories of him and the music he created are touched with sadness. He left an aching emptiness in theatres around the world.

I wish to give here a sincere expression of my homage to him.

15

Singing from the Soul

In the opera world, there's a well-known, unwritten law: Everyone takes second place to the singer. Only a few prominent and charismatic conductors, such as Herbert von Karajan, are exceptions to this rule. This may not be fair, I know, but that's the way it is. Everyone else involved in the production of an opera remains in the shadows.

Nothing much can be done to change the singer's dominant status. He is centre stage. His voice, gestures, and movements convey the drama and command the audience's attention. People today don't go to the theatre just to listen to an opera; they go to see the spectacle itself. The visual aspect of a theatrical production is important, and the growing interest it elicits has been magnified by the rapid development and spread of television.

Many of our predecessors, feeling defensive about the visual impact of their girth, developed the pet theory that a certain bodyweight is required for the voice to sound as it should. I think it's time we admitted, and I'll swear to it, that this rule was advanced as an excuse to overindulge gastronomically and still have a clear conscience. On the other hand, what good is it for a singer to look like a Hollywood lover if he has no voice?

A voice is judged by its volume, inflection, timbre, agility, and range. These are individual qualities which give a singer the means for personal expression, and personal expression is what matters above all else. My goal has always been to project something unique and unmistakable in my voice. If I'm listening to a tenor on the radio and I can't recognize who it is within a few seconds, then he's not an interesting tenor. And I judge sopranos, basses and baritones the same way. When I was a student I loved to compete with my friends in a very entertaining musical game which centred on vocal individuality. One of us would play a passage from a record, and whoever was first to call out the singer's name won a point. If you won the game you were pronounced to have the best ear in the group.

It takes years of training to achieve an unmistakable voice or a trademark style of delivery. Essentially, there are two matters I keep in mind when I sing. In their order of priority they are: to produce the most beautiful sound I can, considering the inherent qualities of my voice, and to use the right technique that helps me correctly and exactly interpret what I'm feeling when I sing. I don't want to place technique ahead of everything else.

Technical craftsmanship alone is not enough in singing. For example, if we must emphasize a difficult passage and a note slips out which is technically less than perfect, we compensate for it by making sure that the words are sung with the exactly right meaning. For me right interpretation is the essential, and everything else is secondary. To concentrate solely on technique is to lose the poetry in the story.

I can illustrate this by citing many singers who have performed for years, but who still give the impression that they've just graduated with honours from the conservatory. Their academic craftsmanship is impressive and that's quite a lot, but if it never evolved into artistry, that's too little. I am not at all impressed by them.

I think that most people now come to the theatre expecting an emotional experience, and in that case technical perfection is no guarantee of a charismatic evening. Naturally, I am aware that it is possible to mesmerize an audience with a fantastic technique, to give them sensational thrills. Why not? Unfortunately, for me that is not enough.

If I am a member of the audience in an opera house, I want the singer onstage to communicate with me. I want his singing to reach all my emotions. I want to feel what he is feeling and to know what he knows. That is exactly why I'm there.

Consequently, when I am on the stage I follow a special formula: from the heart to the mind to the voice. In other words, my heart tells me what to express, it gives listeners all that is within me. My feelings are the driving force up to this point. Then my mind takes over and guides me. "More emphasis here, less there; do this, not that." It shows me how to act a part in a way that best suits me and my goals. Only then does the voice, the vehicle for expression, come into play. With technique, it gives shape to the emotions and the thoughts that I wish to convey.

I call this process *singing from the soul.*

I don't know whether my colleagues agree with me, but this is how I sing. I have to. If I did otherwise, I wouldn't feel I was singing opera. And this is exactly one of our problems today. We have many good singers, but most of them are unable to use their voices to show emotion and to arouse the audience's feelings. I realize that for many listeners the sound and colour of a singer's voice is enough to move them. How much more thrilling it would be if, through a singer's interpretive talent, they could also live the drama and identify with the character.

In this context, it's almost impossible for me to talk about certain colleagues in public, much less judge them. To openly discuss possible rivals leaves a bad taste in my mouth. That's why I won't mention any names, even though I realize I'm perhaps leaving out the juiciest part of the topic.

For instance, I know a few sopranos who fail a note or two with certain regularity or who systematically skip some notes in the score. As far as I'm concerned, I don't mind such practices at all because these women are brilliant interpreters, which more than compensates for a few notes. When I work with them I'm moved deeply by their expressiveness. As my partners they simply carry me away. In this case does a mistake matter? Not in the slightest.

Personally, I think a career without mistakes is boring. Among the errors a singer supposedly makes is to accept a role that seems wrong for the voice. And that is truly a risky business.

I've never been one to sidestep risks. In fact, I've been known to court them in other aspects of my life, off-stage as well. So what if my career is a little shorter because I sing this or that part? I couldn't bear worrying about it every minute. I'll take my chances. I won't be bogged down by a routine career where you settle into comfortable roles that fit your temperament, talent, and voice, dedicating your entire artistic life to a walled-in repertoire. The theory is that you can save your voice long enough to see your rivals collect pensions while you're still on top, performing. No, thanks. I'd find a predictable career hideously boring. My motto is: "Better to sing ten fewer years, but to sing every moment honestly."

Some of my colleagues can produce each note accurately and give the impression that it's all very easy. As you listen to them, everything seems to fit because everything is correct. But does this mean they're musical? Not necessarily. Very often perfection has nothing to do with musicality. Let's say a singer accidentally misses the beat. Off his musical balance, he loses his composure and gets rattled like a metronome in the wind.

Others of my colleagues are so musical, their delivery so absolutely sure and personal, one tends to think they wrote the aria themselves. Nothing and no one can make them lose their confidence and serenity. Even though the purists, those who hold tightly to technique, will find some reasons to criticize their performance, they can never accuse these singers of a bad interpretation.

Finally, there are singers who build each note with precision, controlling it until it sounds exactly the way they want it to sound. They concentrate intensely on the story of the piece and wholeheartedly identify with the role they're singing. I am one of them.

The mental concentration required to give a musically accurate and dramatically valid performance is enormous. Yet to the audience it looks so easy, very natural and very realistic. That, of course, is how it should be. Our tremendous effort shouldn't be obvious. The audience doesn't care how we did it; what matters is the effect.

Sometimes it's even difficult to give them a normal effect. I particularly remember my guest appearance in Budapest at the Erkel Theatre. We were doing Donizetti's *Lucia di Lammermoor,* and everyone in the cast, including the chorus—and even my Lucia, Karola Agai—was singing in Hungarian! Everyone, that is, except me. To be bombarded from all sides by an unfamiliar language was distracting. As I couldn't understand a word my partner was singing, I was forced to sing my entire role without a cue. I tried establishing eye contact with the conductor, hoping to get my cues from him, but the stage manager for *Lammermoori Lucia* (its Hungarian title) had given the chorus strict instructions to keep Edgardo surrounded at all times. So whenever I escaped from the chorus, even for a moment, they were right there again, weaving along with me across the stage and back. I did the only thing I could: I sang everyone's roles in my head. And yet in spite of everything, or perhaps because of everything, it turned out to be a very successful evening for me! I had taken on an unusual challenge, and in spite of the hardships, I still managed to interpret my role. In view of the circumstances, if I hadn't, I'd hope I'd have been forgiven!

Another unforeseen but funny disaster happened at the San Francisco Opera House in 1977. That evening I was singing *Un ballo in maschera*. Katia Ricciarelli and I were in a duet when, much to my bewilderment, Katia began moving away from me, carefully inching her way back toward one of the on-stage pillars. Of course, I followed my Amelia across the stage, trying not to attract attention to our unusual behaviour. Finally Katia whispered, "I'm losing my petticoat!" Concentrating on the music as best we could, we continued singing while Katia, partially hidden by the pillar, struggled to rid herself of the garment that was now down around her knees. But it just wouldn't shake loose.

Fritz, my secretary, was standing in the wings, out of sight of the audience, following the action. Noticing Katia's predicament, he stepped on the edge of the petticoat as it dragged across the floor in front of him. Luckily, the garment stayed behind with Fritz when Katia came back toward me. We were able to finish the scene with no more slip-ups. It was too bad all this had to happen during a musically sensitive passage, but, in spite of the harrowing episode, everything ended well. Later, we were even able to laugh about it.

Again, while singing the same love duet, I had a somewhat less humorous, even more bizarre experience at La Scala in Milan. This time Montserrat Caballé was singing the role of Amelia. On the final note of our duet, Montserrat's voice gave out, and so did mine. Absolutely no sound at all from either of us! Only air! I would rank this a rare moment in operatic history. The audience was positively astounded, which is probably why they treated us as kindly as they did.

This brings me back to certain basic problems faced by the modern opera singer. It's getting more and more difficult for any of us to give what can be called a perfect stage performance. There exist many excellent films, television productions, and studio recordings which represent the ideal in performing arts, and having experienced the best, audiences come to the opera with high expectations and a basis for comparison. But people should be warned: if they expect perfection, they'll be disappointed.

On the stage, perfection is practically impossible to achieve. Yet if we can project across the footlights the spontaneity and immediacy of live performance rather than just correctly sung notes, I believe the majority of opera-goers will settle for less than ideal results. This, of course, doesn't mean that we should stop striving for that ideal.

I still remember the days when I was an avid opera-goer and how we used to discuss the singers and compare them. What violent arguments we had in our standing room only crowd! It is not unusual for a group of fans to respect and adore and almost deify a particular singer while others think him simply abominable. In my case, the mystery of such bias is easily explained. There has always been a special type of performer, who by his art could move me.

Let's see if I can describe this better. When I was young I'd hear a singer and think, "He is singing for me and for me alone." Something would click, something would stir deep within me, and I would become a devoted fan. Here I have to bring up Di Stefano's name again. A long time ago, this great tenor reached into my heart with his "Che gelida manina." It was just three words, but his sensitive rendition, the "how" of his singing, filled my whole being in a way no other singer ever did before.

To be won over by someone's voice, I needed to be deeply moved. Otherwise, at best, I could do no more than admire the amazing vocal technique of some of our great opera stars. But to *love* a voice, I had to discover the singer's heart and soul in it. This is how I've always felt, and the passing years have not changed my values.

Since feelings are highly individual, a universal standard by which to value a singer isn't possible. Everyone is free, luckily, to vote for his favourite as the "ideal" singer.

Sometimes I get the distinct feeling there are people in the theatre who think that opera is a circus. For them the tenor is some kind of trapeze artist (and at times, also a clown). They sit on the proverbial edge of their seats, wishing and waiting for him to do a triple somersault instead of his regular double flips. And the higher and more spectacular the evening's triple somersault is, the better they like it. The audience's anticipation for that one fantastic, soaring note, the coveted high C, hangs over a tenor's head particularly during an opera the public knows well. This doesn't happen during performances of less known works, as no one expects a high C, if they don't know that one is coming.

I suppose it's unavoidable that we singers will be compared. The truth is, I don't like the competition. It turns art into a sporting event, in which bookmakers take bets. What's worse, comparisons are made between singers who don't appear together and are not of the same time periods. It's sort of a duel at a distance. Obviously, comparison, no matter how contrived, has become the mark of today's society, in which everyone likes to speak in superlatives: "The greatest!" "The most beautiful!" "The best!" I wish these labels were banned from opera, but I suppose that's asking for the impossible.

In my opinion there are three types of opera fans: first, those who come to hear the high notes and care little about anything else; next, those who love the great and powerful voice and couldn't care less about what is sung or how it's sung; and finally, those who prize what we call "style" in singing.

Of course, the ideal would be to find all three qualities in one person: a refined singer with a gigantic voice who can belt out incredibly high notes, a marvellous combination, but an impossible dream. At least, I've yet to meet this phenomenon of nature and training. On the other hand, it's necessary to have at least one of the three qualities to have a chance of a career in opera.

As a listener, I'm not at all interested in a tenor whose only saving grace is that he can crown the *stretta* in *Il trovatore* with a dazzling high C. If he ignores the subtleties of "Ah si, ben mio," glosses over the piano and legato markings, or yells his way through the final trio, he has lost me.

Let's stop for a moment and delve into the *stretta* from *Il trovatore* and the razzle-dazzle of its high C ending. It's a problem. This *stretta* is a prime example of what could be called "schizophrenia" in opera literature, as it has lost contact over the years with the realities of the original composition. When Verdi created the role of Manrico, he wrote a score that was a "tenor's delight." The highest note was an A, a piece of cake for tenors who find the high C hard to scale. This is the majority of cases. But along the way, I don't know how or when, it became the custom to top off this *stretta* with a high C. In fact, this note may have turned into the most famous high C in the literature of opera. The audience can hardly wait for it to come while most tenors can hardly wait to get it over with. Public anticipation intensifies the strain on most singers, and this pressure is worst during such perennial blockbusters as "La donna e mobile," "Che gelida manina," and many others. In fact, this is the very reason why a tenor misses that high note when it finally comes, or worse, spoils the rest of the aria. Today this can become a professional calamity. One can lose more by botching up a *stretta* than gain by having an otherwise fabulous evening. Once, when this problem was being discussed in our circle of professional friends someone bantered that the *Il trovatore* posters in front of the opera house should advertise "*Stretta* With the High C!" or "*Stretta* Without the High C!" Then fans could take their choice.

In spite of everything, I'm convinced that the majority of opera fans are now coming to the theatre to see how an artist does during the whole performance, not just when he is showcased in certain arias. After all, we have to sing every note in the score, not only those which are the most convenient or those which the composer never wrote.

16

The Winning Hand: Programmes and Conductors

I THINK THAT singers find their moment of truth more in the concert hall than in the opera house. I confess that I love to give concerts. I mean that I love to offer programmes with universal appeal and to sing arias or fragments from operas that everyone can hum. Such evenings of communion between the singer and the audience hold their own special enchantment for me. A performer, especially a tenor, can "set the house on fire" (if things go well), because there's always that segment of the public that couldn't care less about unknown material. They will ask for and be pleased only by the same favourite old tunes.

At a recital the singer is seen under vastly different circumstances than in an opera performance. When I sing in an opera, I'm sheltered within the sets and surrounded by my colleagues. I'm supported by the orchestra and the conductor who guides me from the pit. I'm in character, costumed, made up for my part and, in the worst of cases, wearing a wig (an accessory for which I have little love). In

147

addition I'm in continuous dramatic action, moving about as necessary.

But in a concert or song recital, things are quite different. I am alone. My place is fixed: centre stage, next to the piano and my sole companion is the pianist. Although I'm dressed in tails, I feel naked. In compensation, however, I feel that I'm giving my all to the audience in a very forceful manner. The great attraction of such an evening is that each song represents, as it were, its own world. Each composer and each style offers something rare and different to the listeners. This variety gives me a unique chance to prepare a programme that bears my own individual stamp: I'm able to select pieces that best suit my vocal possibilities and temperament, and allow me to win the public with my voice and my power of expression.

Yet, as positive an experience giving a recital can be, it is fraught with some serious problems. For example, in opera performances a small mistake frequently goes unnoticed, but in a recital it's not only caught immediately, it's further magnified beyond all proportions by the cognoscenti in the audience.

I prefer a certain type of programme, which consists of romantic and melancholy pieces. Why do I choose such material? For the obvious reason, I'm a romantic person, touched with melancholy. The feelings in these songs are close to my nature and personality, and I'm able to interpret them much more truthfully than I do the so-called light music. This has nothing to do with its quality, but with my personal tendencies as an interpreter.

Naturally, since I favour romantic music, I prefer to portray the great romantic characters of opera. I am, and will remain, a lyric tenor, even though I have also sung another type of tenor role: the *lirico-spinto*, which combines the lyric with the dramatic. Such are the roles of Don Carlos, Andrea Chenier, Don José, Alvaro, et al. I have interpreted them very successfully, and they too are a part of my repertoire.

The differences in role types don't affect the way I learn an opera, for when I'm handed a new score all my personal biases fade into secondary considerations. Usually, I'm a quick learner. First, I go over the score with my pianist; then, I determine the best way to approach the role, musically and dramatically.

The musical and technical aspects of Verdi and Donizetti pose no major problems or hidden dangers for me, and I can learn these works in just a few days. The difficulty lies elsewhere, for it is necessary to give each role the right expression and, consequently, the proper dynamics. After all, the process of building a part is more than just singing the notes correctly.

Even if you judge that you've developed a most stirring interpretation, your work isn't finished. Far from it. You can't sing a role precisely the same way forever. On the contrary, there's a natural progression. The stage proves to be a good teacher; you uncover new dimensions in the work that continually enrich your characterization.

No matter how much you learn by repeating a new part with your pianist, from beginning to end ten times over, it's not enough. Once on stage, you discover how difficult it is to do everything right! The difference between piano rehearsals and actual performance is appalling. Suddenly there's the sound and volume of an orchestra to contend with, your colleagues around you, and you must coordinate your work with them. Sometimes, to stay on the track and avoid any possible pitfalls later on, it's necessary to become completely familiar with the musical side of all the other roles as well.

An audience often believes that the most difficult thing for a singer is to avoid being unsettled and losing his bearings when his colleagues are singing something totally different. I must say that this was never a problem for me. After all, we're all singing in harmony, only we join in at different moments and in different musical intervals. We have to remain musically united with our singing counterparts. And here we discover who is a good singer and who is not. The bad singer pushes on pigheadedly, ignoring everyone else, not really listening, while a truly musical performer will be able to adjust spontaneously yet appropriately to his partners anywhere in the action. He doesn't need to count time in his head and, therefore, won't act like a machine.

With a good conductor, many problems can easily be avoided. Under solid leadership we can't lose ourselves; we keep the beat and are spared all sorts of sudden musical catastrophes. Spectators who aren't trained in music don't usually notice the discrepancies that can develop between the conductor in the pit and the performers on stage.

Nevertheless, the most absurd and frenzied situations can occur when someone, either in the orchestra or on stage, loses his control. I've seen enraged sopranos attack an incompetent conductor, at intermission or after the final curtain. Swearing on their dead relatives, the divas vow never to work with that musician again! I've also heard indignant maestros explode with abuse, cursing a singer who shows no self-discipline. At La Scala I even witnessed a scuffle.

But these are exceptions. When a singer works with a great conductor there are few incidents worth mentioning. The label "great" is well justified. These maestros' interpretations of the works are more important to the artists and the public than any anecdotes that document whims, blunders, desertions, and other such rubbish. Whether it's Karajan or Bernstein, Abbado or Muti, Kleiber or Maazel, Giulini or Levine, to mention just a few, each has charisma. Yet not one of them really possesses a "secret." They're simply men with overwhelming personalities who are exceptionally musical and in complete artistic command of their profession.

When a conductor of this calibre raises his baton, the orchestra produces a better sound as each musician concentrates more intensely on his work. This concentration and rapport carries over to the chorus and the soloists on the stage. The effect is fascinating. We singers are spurred on by the marvellous playing of the orchestra, and, in turn, the orchestra responds with still greater fire. We call this interaction "creative tension." And the architect of all this brilliance is the truly great maestro. Unfortunately, there are only a few such conductors in our time.

While singing Verdi's *Requiem Mass*, I found out how wonderful it is to work with great maestros and how they differ in their interpretations. In the whole literature of music, the *Requiem* happens to be one of my favourite works. Verdi once declared, "We already have too many masses for the dead. There is no need to add another." We can be grateful that he changed his mind and composed one of the most powerful masses in Italian music. I wish to state for the record that I don't agree with the general viewpoint that it's an "opera for the dead" and, therefore, a markedly theatrical work. There's nothing theatrical about the *Requiem*, but it is intensely dramatic. The difference between these two concepts is enormous. Verdi may have been the first composer to endow a religious work with certain dramatic elements normally found in opera.

I was lucky enough to perform the *Requiem* several

times under the four great conductors of our time, Herbert von Karajan, Carlo Maria Giulini, Claudio Abbado, and Riccardo Muti. Working with each one was a completely different experience. I first learned the tenor part in the *Requiem* for Karajan, in Salzburg. My debut was with Mirella Freni, Fiorenza Cossotto, and Nicolai Ghiaurov. Later I sang it with Anna Tomowa-Sintow, Agnes Baltsa, and José van Dam. When I worked with Giulini, the soloists were Katia Ricciarelli, Brigitte Fassbaender and Ruggero Raimondi. Then I performed for Abbado with Margaret Price, Jessye Norman, and Ruggero Raimondi. Finally, my turn came with Riccardo Muti, and my colleagues were once more Jessye Norman, Agnes Baltsa, and Raimondi.

It was an accident that brought me to Muti. I had been singing at the Vienna Staatsoper in *Lucia* when on the eve of a performance I received a telephone call from the Maestro. He wanted me to substitute for the indisposed Veriano Lucchetti. I agreed immediately, and that same night I travelled to Munich. Next morning we had just enough time for one piano rehearsal. But in spite of last-minute madness, the concert turned out very well. Later Muti and I worked together again, this time in Florence, where my colleagues were Elizabeth Connell, Agnes Baltsa, and Kurt Rydll.

I am not a critic. I won't offer an opinion as to which Maestro was the best conductor for me or which orchestra was better than the other. Establishing an order of preference is strictly a matter of personal taste. Each of the four interpretations was excellent in its own way, and an unforgettable experience for me. Karajan achieved a tremendous depth through the interplay of dynamics and orchestral colours; he made me feel that this was how the great composer had intended the work to sound.

Abbado's approach was cerebral, his interpretation intellectual. Muti, above all else, infused the *Requiem* with a fiery passion while Giulini's reading was the most introverted. Each of the four versions was different, yet each Maestro was able to successfully communicate to the listeners the intuitive and the mystical qualities of this colossal work.

These four conductors are inseparably linked with my role in the *Messa da Requiem*. When I think of this work I think of Karajan, Giulini, Abbado, and Muti. My experience with them was like holding all four aces, if I may use the analogy, each one a winner in its own right and, together, the unbeatable hand of my career.

Overleaf.
A conductor who is an excellent accompanist: Riccardo Muti plays the piano during a benefit concert in Ravenna.

A conductor who is an excellent accompanist: Riccardo Muti plays the piano during a benefit concert in Ravenna.

17

The Play's the Thing

To be an actor or a singer takes a certain streak of exhibitionism. The mere act of stepping in front of an audience should be a pleasure. Anyone who suffers just at the thought of appearing in public will very quickly give up his career. This is equally true of someone who has the floor during a business conference or who is delivering a speech before a large audience. Have you ever watched a group of children as they recite a poem? Some of them perform with real enthusiasm and fervor while others would prefer to sink into the first hole in the ground.

I'm basically an introvert, and singing is an anomalous trait in my personality makeup. Singing changes me. It allows me to open up completely. Not only that, as I come out of my shell, I go even beyond the usual limits of an extrovert. I can give my all and reveal my most intimate feelings.

A theatrical performance is different. With drama, on stage, I have a constant fear that I'm doing too much. There's a tenuous, barely perceived boundary between acting a part with intense dramatic truth and the cheap spectacle of being a ham. A certain kind of garish display may impress a large number of spectators, but it goes against my grain. Even if it were the way to success, I'd consider it worthless, as long as it prevented me from knowing who I am or, worse, from being true to myself.

There's an imaginary door which I never open. Even if the brain orders me to do so, there's an indefinable mechanism which clicks into place and prevents me from obeying. It's not only a facet of natural shyness, but a matter of character, and I can neither deny nor contradict my own feelings.

After all, the essential in opera is singing and musical interpretation. These two elements depend to a large degree on how cooperative are the other members of the cast. In a duet, for instance, it's truly fantastic when the soprano reacts exactly as I expect at any given moment. It enables me to respond to her precisely in the way that I want to. And it's the most frustrating thing in the whole opera world when such give and take doesn't happen. I give her my all. Expression. Words. Music. Everything meshes, allowing me to produce a perfect sound. Meantime the soprano just stands there, giving nothing of herself, alienated from all the emotion that I have aimed at her, or at least at the character she portrays, somehow completely self-absorbed, as if she were somewhere in space. At this point, all interaction ceases. There's nothing, absolutely nothing, that I can find to give her back.

I must admit that the ideal situation, this symbiosis that moves the spectators and packs the theatres, occurs only rarely. In 1978, as Alvaro in *La forza del destino* at La Scala, I had one such supreme moment. Piero Cappuccilli was as phenomenal an adversary as I could wish for. Everything simply flowed, timed exactly with all my expectations. Each phrase came precisely when I wanted to hear it, enabling my voice to yield the exact response. It was a continuous give-and-take with maximum results. Such a fulfilment is an artist's dream. To sense instinctively what your partner will do next allows you to form a very definite response. Everything develops naturally, as it should. In singing, these responses can't be learned or rehearsed. They happen spontaneously, arising from the singers and the circumstances of each particular evening. And, surprisingly, it's far easier to achieve this empathy between battling antagonists than between stage lovers.

However, I remember an exception to this rule when I sang my first Canio in Madrid in the 1986 production of Leoncavallo's *I pagliacci*. My Nedda, Ilona Tokody, was an ideal partner. Her reactions to my bursts of anger were so brilliant and transformed Canio's feelings into such rage that I continued to give even more of myself to the part than I ever had before. In my opinion, Ilona Tokody is an ideal interpreter of verismo roles. Here I have to emphasize that what I describe as symbiosis or interaction has nothing to do with creating stage effects. To sing for effect only involves no special art. Any opera fan who pays close attention will realize that musically unmotivated effects are achieved at the expense of notes.

Unfortunately, audiences get caught up in these "special effects." We have a perfect example in the finale of *La Bohème* when Rodolfo realizes that Mimi has died. A tenor who sobs, whimpers, and cries probably impresses the majority of spectators who, in this tragic moment, have already been swayed by their feelings. But Rodolfo's histrionics aren't required by the libretto, nor did Puccini foresee any spectacular outpouring of grief. The tenor doesn't need to add any emotion, it's all in the music. If I can't express Rodolfo's pain with my voice, then, I'm obviously not a good tenor.

There's another operatic special effect that I consider to be even worse than just being a ham on stage, and that's including notes that are not in the score. I don't believe this out of personal convenience, because I'm not exactly a high note specialist, but because I think they're musically unsuitable, in most cases, and against the wishes of the composer. If a tenor fancies that at the end of the duet with Posa in *Don Carlos* or at the conclusion of the love duet in the Nile scene of *Aida* he must sing a high C, then there's no way to help him. The man has no understanding or feeling for the score.

By way of a final example, I can cite one tenor situation that is truly comical in its effect, the crowing outbursts of laughter repeatedly thrown into "E scherzo od e follia" from *Un ballo in maschera*. In some of the old records, the piece sounds more like a parody of singing than an actual aria. Yet what Verdi composed for this scene is completely sufficient. The original music is all we need.

18

Fame

Over the years, society has changed in many ways and so have the singers. Gone are the days when we were untouchable and unapproachable. We no longer stand on imaginary pedestals, gazing with pleasure and condescension at the opera world lying at our feet. We don't want to be surrounded by a mystical aura. For some tenors it was once necessary, and inevitable, to parade their fame in chauffeur-driven limousines or mark it with extravagant behaviour even outside the theatre. But those days are now history.

Actually, the artists were not completely at fault. Their public expected them to attract attention, to be exalted and adventurous, even tainted by a hint of scandal. And if the "divo" had only a few eccentricities, then at least it was necessary to exhibit a fetish or two.

In the world of opera, it's the easiest thing to do. I'd merely have to mention, just a few times and with proper persistence, that I can only sing when I see a flowering cactus in the prompter's box. Immediately, all my biographical resumés would be updated to include the following quote: "This is the tenor who is most hated by prompters, for during his performances they always get pricked by cactus."

No, this isn't my style. I leave such bizarre behaviour to colleagues who constantly need to reassure themselves of their star status. True, the whole world has quirks, but I'd rather keep mine to myself. One of my habits is to nurse a drink of water before a performance—not very spectacular of me and certainly not something I give out as my registered trademark.

I hold that the only place to act like a "star" is at the rehearsal, to be the first and not the last to arrive, or at least to be punctual; to be completely prepared, disciplined, and perform without antics or mood swings. I believe these traits characterize a true professional, which is what a star should be, nothing more. I know that years ago there was a different mentality. "I'm a star. Let the others wait." Now we work in a more professional way, and at the same time we are friendlier toward each other. Old rivalries between tenors and prima donnas, filled with hate, baseness, envy, and deceit, are in the past. Although today opera singers aren't exactly a family of brothers and sisters living in perfect harmony, their spirit of cooperation and camaraderie has vastly improved.

I'm very happy that today we have a chance to lead a completely normal life. For example, after the performance I discard my costume and become just another citizen like everyone else. By the way, my colleagues who insist that it takes hours to shed their dramatic "persona" are fibbing at times. I like to go about in jeans and a T-shirt without anyone turning up his nose at me. But it wouldn't matter if they did. When the mood hits me I enjoy going to a football game or seeing a film. And when I decide to go shopping I like to carry my own bags to the hotel. In other words, I like to live simply and unnoticed. But my position as an artist keeps me in the centre of public attention, and I can't escape the fuss, inconvenient at times as it might be.

I don't say that being popular is annoying. It makes me very happy when someone recognizes me in the street or a restaurant or a shop. But I want to emphasize that I don't try to be recognized. In fact, I would be perfectly comfortable if I were anonymous. To be enslaved by one's own status is irritating, especially when one is already a slave to one's profession.

As far as popularity is concerned, opera singers can't compare with the superstars of sports, film, or pop music. Thank God, because I couldn't live in a glass house like Diego Maradona, Boris Becker, Robert Redford, or Michael Jackson. They can't make a move without being noticed and discussed in the press. For them, a private life is only possible behind locked gates.

I value being a celebrity in the world of opera because it's a smaller, more encompassed community. After every performance in any theatre, I find familiar faces among the regular fans who wait at the stage door. And since I have a good memory, I clearly recognize them. Sometimes I can even spot them from the stage. These pleasant people are a different breed from fans who are found in sports arenas; they seem so happy when I stop and chat with them that I do it with pleasure.

Even after the most strenuous evening, I'm not disturbed to find friends and acquaintances at my dressing room, exactly the opposite! If one day I opened the door and found no one I'd feel that something was just not right, even though it would mean I could go peacefully straight home. To me these visitors are emissaries of public opinion, and their reactions to my performance interest me more than the published reviews.

Of course, there's always the friend or acquaintance

who can never say, "Sorry to tell you this, but tonight you were bad." Fortunately, there are others who will. And when a friend whose judgement I trust says nothing, this too has meaning. Silence can speak loudly. What I don't need is a room full of flatterers who assure me how well I've done. At this point I may become less than polite because I distrust anyone who is amiable at all times and claims to appreciate the whole world. There's something unnatural and absurd about a person who is pleased by everyone and everything. That's why I'm very selective about the people who surround me. When the opera is over, I'd rather focus on different topics instead of analyzing every note, phrase, and incident of the performance. And that kind of under-standing and intimacy are only possible within a small circle of friends.

Friendship is one of the best gifts in life. In my position it is sometimes difficult to tell who is sincere and who is not. There are people who want to be close to a famous tenor because it makes them important. There are those who simply want to use me. If an artist doesn't have the sense to know the difference, who does? Although at times I can be fooled, my typical Catalan upbringing helps to spare me such errors and their consequences. My formula is first wait and see, then test and retest. Never let anyone come near until you believe you're sure of him. Just as there's love at first sight, there can be friendship at first sight, but this is rare.

On the other hand, I've met people whom I instinc-tively distrusted after just a few minutes of conversation. Something warned me against them. And generally it doesn't take long to confirm the truth of my feelings.

Fan mail is a totally different relationship. Why should someone whom I personally don't know and will probably never meet take the trouble to flatter me? I receive tens of thousands of letters each year, and ninety-nine point nine percent are delightful. They are friendly, sympathetic, enthusiastic, full of good advice, emotional and even poetic, all that one can imagine. My greatest joy comes from letters that are written in simple, heartfelt words: "When I hear your voice, I feel better" or "Hearing you makes me happy".

At the risk of sounding melodramatic, let me ask you if there is anything more rewarding than practicing a profession which you love above all else and which allows you to give a sense of happiness and well-being to others?

Overleaf.
As Rodolfo, in *La Bohème*, the Met, 1982. Looking out over Parisian rooftops. It was a new production designed and directed by Franco Zeffirelli.

19

New Productions, Audience Behaviour

Curious opera fans always want to know the decisive factors in choosing an opera for a new production. Do the top singers always get what they want? Who makes final decisions, the Artistic Director or the conductor? Is it true that for some time now the directors of the great opera houses feel they have lost their power? That they can only push their ideas through with outside help?

I believe there's some truth in all these suppositions. Certain singers will always demand and get certain roles. Famous stage directors and important orchestra leaders have complete trust of their admiring patrons, who lavish unlimited financial backing on their projects. Yet even in this ideal situation, results can fall short of expectations. The best terms in a contract do not necessarily guarantee final success; it can happen that the most prestigious singers are sometimes miscast. On the other hand, all of us have seen wonderful productions which succeeded very well without the benefit of famous names.

Basically, then, each director is judged by the productions mounted during his tenure at the opera house. He's

also assessed as to whether he has any qualities of a Zeffirelli or a Strehler and whether he can command better
and more spectacular casts than his predecessor or his
competition in the other great houses.

Faced with these comparisons, expectations, and
judgments, what programme will a new director venture
upon? Well, if he can afford it, he'll form an illustrious team
of name singers and assemble the best possible casts to support them. Unfortunately, few theatres have the budget
necessary to mount such high-powered and noteworthy
productions. Even if money is available, stage directors
may have a difficult time marshalling brilliant casts, as
there's only a handful of "stars" to go round.

Unlike some of my colleagues, I wouldn't accept every
new production that comes along, even if I had the time and
it was technically feasible to do so. I don't wish to spend my
life as a singer doing experiments or wasting my time with
dull, second-rate stage directors who throw away weeks
teaching me such trivialities as where to put my right foot in
a particular scene. I always need to feel that my actions on
stage are meaningful; otherwise, I prefer to stick with the
repertory that's already on the boards.

Naturally, new productions are a legitimate artistic
"must" and not just a gambit for prestige. It's necessary to
renew certain great works to satisfy the audiences' love of
them and to maintain our own high standards as performers. Working with the best conductors and the best stage directors, even occasionally, keeps us on our toes. You just
can't compare *La Bohème* led by Karajan and the same opera
under another competent but not outstanding conductor.
Someone like Karajan forced you to stretch, to give your
best. With him a singer learned so much that every lesson
was ultimately brought to good use in many other roles and
productions.

I love the nervous excitement, the energy, that surrounds a premiere. Not that a revival lacks in atmosphere, but the mood is perceptibly different. Whoever says that opening night jitters disappear after several years' experience either cheats himself or doesn't understand what the whole process is about. Actually, each performance grows harder and harder since everyone expects more from a singer as time increases his fame. At the beginning of a career you can improve daily and add to your knowledge. Afterwards, it can be exactly the opposite; you can lose a great deal in a twinkling of an eye.

New productions are important because they keep you from stagnating in comfortable routines, which is otherwise almost inevitable. The most beautiful stage picture can turn old hat, and any role you've sung a hundred times or more needs an infusion of new blood. But without distortions. I happen to have strong doubts about directors who try to force an avant garde effect, which usually ends in radical excesses. At the risk of being called old-fashioned or conservative, I reject such ridiculous productions.

Obviously, each composer builds his opera on a dramatic situation, and the music presupposes a libretto. However, this doesn't give the stage director the right to degrade, or even ignore, the music. There are productions in which the complete work of art that is an opera becomes nothing more than a theatrical evening with musical accompaniment. If I'm handed a thick notebook full of stage directions for a work that successfully lasted a century without an instructions manual I lose interest. I don't even want to see such a production, much less be associated with it in any way.

A few years ago, I caught a television report on a new staging of *Aida* at the Frankfurt Opera. Radames must have been an archeologist because he dug up a skull next to his desk. Holding it in his hand like Hamlet, he started to sing "Celeste Aida." Then I saw Aida—and she was the cleaning woman. That's all I could take, and I turned off the TV. It wasn't only silly and ridiculous, the production was an offense to Verdi! The stage director had reduced the musical dimensions of this masterpiece to mere accompaniment. My impression was that he had no desire to create a work for the theatre; his interest was in headlines.

I don't mind intellectual games as long as they are based on reason and never rob the music of its meaning. Beyond this point, the action simply becomes eccentric and serves to feed the egotism of certain snobs. Some stage directors resort to scandal as the only way to draw attention to their productions. As a result, within a few weeks after the opening, no one talks about the opera any more, but it continues to haunt the house with serious consequences. The production, having cost lots of money, has to be paid off and is performed for years, an ordeal for the public and the singers. When an irate Piero Cappuccilli left a production of *Rigoletto* in Florence before it opened, there were fireworks. Piero withdrew because the stage director wanted him to appear as a clown. A huge scandal ensued, and the press blasted my friend with all sorts of criticisms. Later he told me there were scenes in which the portrayal so crudely violated the music that Piero simply couldn't agree with it.

For me modern theatre means something more than turning a work "upside down" or updating it to a present-day setting. Jean-Pierre Ponnelle (who unfortunately died in the summer of 1988) showed by his exciting staging of *Carmen* in Zurich how an opera can be both traditional and at the same time modern. The creative power of this imaginative and intelligent director of our time was simply fascinating. He enlivened his staging with original and meaningful details based on keen psychological observations. When fans who know *Carmen* by heart are sitting on the edge of their seats, overtaken by the tension released on stage, the director has succeeded in making theatre in the best sense of the word.

I remember with pleasure and pride the *Carmen* which was presented in the Herodes Atticus, the most famous theatre of Athens. That evening the Ponnelle concept blended so well with the ageless atmosphere of the place that my dear colleague, Agnes Baltsa, and I were overwhelmed by the experience. It was indeed one of the high points of our careers.

In producing opera one must also consider the interaction between the audience and the performer. It's an essential component of every great operatic happening. Any singer can tell you how difficult it is to perform when the public is tired or distracted. In fact a physically exhausted audience is one of the greatest problems in the theatre. Ideally, spectators should come in refreshed and relaxed, having read at leisure the libretto and listened to a recording of the work. The person who has worked all day in a stressful environment can hardly follow a live spectacle with any concentration. Nor can he read a book or get involved in a meaningful film, for that matter. At most, he can sustain a superficial conversation, ending the evening in front of his television set.

It's the same old story. An opera-goer races home after a strenuous day, slips into fresh clothes like a quick-change artist, and sets out in bumper-to-bumper traffic. Arriving at the opera at the last moment, he rushes in with his tongue hanging out, hurriedly searches for his tickets, leaves his coat in the cloakroom, gets his programme, and finally, exhausted, collapses into his seat. He won't even scan the programme until he goes home.

If the performance is a heavy Wagnerian epic our hapless spectator has had it. He suffers. If he lives in the South
of Europe, he may be able to have a little rest between work
and the theatre because there curtain time is traditionally
later in the evening. But this is true only in the best of cases,
as the working day is frequently extended until curtain
time.

The solution is in the artists' hands. We have to involve
the spectators, get them interested, and pull them into the
magic of the theatre. It's not always an easy task, but it's our
duty and it can be done. After all, their visit to the opera
should be a pleasure.

It's not often that a busy singer finds a moment to attend a performance. When this happens, I obviously see
with different eyes and hear with different ears than others
in the audience. I admit it's simply impossible for me to follow an opera, content and relaxed in my seat, enjoying the
music and the voices. Rather the opposite happens. And if I
am relaxed and distracted, it's a sign that the performance
is weak. When the production is good, I live it intensely,
unconsciously externalizing my feelings. Once at La Scala,
a long-suffering lady tapped me twice on the shoulder to
make me finally sit still. I was getting on her nerves.

A visit to the opera is always a learning experience for
me. When I find myself in the auditorium looking up at the
place where I would normally be singing I try to think like a
member of the public. If my expectations and hopes aren't
fulfilled I see what doesn't work and what the singer should
do to make it work. Or I discover things which I immediately promise myself that I'll never do. It may also happen
that I react with an "Aha, so this passage sounds much better soft!" Naturally, in this respect the tenor holds most of

my interest, especially if he's singing a part in my repertoire.

When a singer becomes a listener it's like being in the
arena. There are only two choices: to be the bullfighter or
the bull. One can empathize with a fellow singer and trust
that it'll all come out well for him. One works with him,
breathes with him, and swears at the conductor who
changes *tempi* as if the singer had the air supply of a deep sea
diver. And one prays for him when he gets to that certain
passage, the high point of the role.

The other choice is to sit there, hostile, with the secret
hope that the singer flops. In his heart, this special breed of
spectator is at peace only when he decides that he could
have done it better. He listens to the applause the other
tenor earns, and if it is shorter and less fervent than what he
usually gets he feels reassured.

I don't believe that a half-way normal person could
hope that another singer will miss a note or fail in some
other way and be jeered by the crowd. For me this is almost
as bad as wishing that someone be run over by a car. I always
hope that my colleagues do well, even if they are presumed
to be my greatest rivals. I know only too well how difficult it
is to be up there alone.

Those who don't know are, without a doubt, the
"booers." For me they're pitiful creatures whose psychological mechanisms aren't quite well-tuned, to put it
kindly. Arriving at the theatre with the intention of being
actively involved in the performance, they consider themselves to be one of its integral elements. Their role is that of
agitators who want to proclaim by shouting that their understanding is deeper than the combined audience's applause and bravos.

Once I had the chance to talk to one of these negative
booers. He was quite a young man, and it soon became ap-

parent that he was deplorably ignorant. The performance hadn't been to his liking, he confided, but when he tried to quote me some examples his incompetence reached even greater proportions. Such people can't be helped, they jumble everything and abuse the right of free speech. It's true that everyone can have and proclaim his own viewpoint, but no one is the sole arbiter of truth, and no one has the right to protest disruptively just because a singer was not on target in satisfying someone's individual taste.

Of course, there are people who simply have to disagree with everything. But booing? Usually there's a dubious motive for it. For a spectator to lose his control because of a failed high note, loss of tone, or any other musical mishap on stage is not only unfair but shows a total lack of sensitivity and respect for another human being. After all, an accidental mistake can happen to anyone. But the worst opera "friends" are those who, out of misguided love for their favourite, boo all the other singers whom they deem in competition. I find this behaviour obnoxious.

Protesting is legitimate in only the circumstance when the artist isn't prepared or has done so very poorly. It shows a serious lack of professional responsibility when a singer doesn't do everything in his or her power to master the role. Such conduct should not be tolerated. Besides it's a fraud against the paying public. No one should be expected to shell out full price for a half-finished product.

20

The Critics

ONE OF the headiest experiences a young singer can have when starting his career is when he sees for the first time his name in the newspapers. One sentence of praise or perhaps a picture are enough to fire his imagination. Walking down the street, he believes that every passerby recognizes him, thinking, "Look! There goes that new tenor who was so great in the opera last night." Obviously there's no logic in the excited beginner's reasoning; nevertheless, I agree that performers should not underestimate the power of critics. For example, my debut at the New York City Opera caused Harold Schonberg, the eminent critic of *The New York Times*, to note that I was "really something extraordinary." Perhaps that was reason enough for the movers and shakers of the opera world to sit up and take notice. This one good review may have encouraged them to check me out, to listen to me, hire me, and recommend me to others. Who knows, anything is possible!

Over the years, I've learned to live with criticism. In time, I even learned to make distinctions in the barrage of words aimed at me. There will always be critics who praise you to the skies, no matter what you do. There are other reviewers whose approval seesaws, like the weather. In the

negative case, you'd love to think that the critic is mistaken.
Yet there's a nagging doubt at the back of your mind, "Is it
possible that during that particular recital or performance
I wasn't up to par?"

Then there is that third type of critic, who doesn't care
how you're singing or what you're singing. His mind is all
made up, even before you open your mouth. These reviews
have little to do with the actual performance, and para-
graphs are filled with insinuations and misrepresenta-
tions, punctuated with marginal and spiteful remarks. We
all have a few such friends on the staff of certain newspapers. Some of them studied music but failed to make it their
career, and this perhaps explains their frustrated, negative
attitude. I learned a long time ago, "There's no use in worrying. It's all part of the game."

Don't believe singers who claim not to read their press.
They lie. When a bad review hits the streets, annoyance is
your first reaction. After twenty-four hours, both the
words and your temper fade into the sunset. There's nothing so stale and boring as yesterday's news. If you see the
review a few days later, the initial anger that you felt has already been muted. All this doesn't mean that you can't
learn something from a negative review, as long as it is written by a good reviewer. Karajan told me once, "If you believe the good reviews, then you must believe the bad ones,
too!"

In the United States, the press can be a nightmare. Every issue is exaggerated, and there are times when I feel that
Americans seem to need someone to shape their opinions.
This is certainly true of politics where their press is part of
the decisionmaking process. However, a glance at New
York's Broadway proves that music and drama do not with-
stand journalistic influence either. Suppose a new musical
opens, and its cost is astronomical, well into the millions of

My house debut at La Scala, as Riccardo in *Un ballo in maschera*, 1975. Giuseppe di Stefano gifted me with this costume. It now has a place of honour in my house.

Giuseppe di Stefano, the idol of my youth and my great tenor model.

Here we are just before the premiere of *Andrea Chenier* at La Scala in Milan, on December 23, 1982.

With Maestro Herbert von Karajan: in the middle of a rehearsal for the 1982 recording of *Carmen* in Berlin. Below : As Rodolfo in *Luisa Miller,* the Met, 1982. Eleven years earlier, Rodolfo's romanza had been one of the two arias that had helped me to get through the preliminaries in the 1971 Verdi Competition, which I eventually won.

In 1984, with Maestro Lorin Maazel, one-time director of the Vienna Opera. The occasion: my receiving the title of Kammersänger.

Our conductor Riccardo Chailly, Piero Cappuccilli, and me after the 1982 premiere of *Andrea Chenier* in Milan.

With Rudolf Schock and Anna Moffo in a television program in Dortmund.

Relaxing in the San Francisco sunshine, 1973. It was a time when everything was new and, caught up in my enthusiasm, I was ready for any challenge. Left, my San Francisco Opera house debut: as Rodolfo in *La Bohème*, with Teresa Stratas. I love playing the young poet because he elicits affection and understanding. To show love, jealousy, misery, hope and despair, all in one evening is an irresistible challenge for a tenor.

My first time at the Met, as Cavaradossi in *Tosca*, 1974. This and other prestigious house debuts—Vienna Staatsoper, London's Royal Opera, the Munich National Theatre—resulted from my success at the smaller New York City Opera.

Two of my roles in the San Francisco Opera: my first American Nemorino, with Judith Blegen as Adina, *L'elisir d'amore,* in 1975, and Riccardo, *Un ballo in maschera,* 1977. A still from this production became the jacket of the recording I made for Philips. A favourite opera of mine, it is associated with important moments in my life—including the births of my children.

As Cavaradossi
in one of my
many *Toscas* at
the Metropolitan
Opera.

Rehearsing *Aida,*
Salzburg, 1979, with
Maestro Karajan. He
believed in consistency
between stage action
and music.

My first opera for
Karajan was *Don Carlos*
in 1976. I created this
role many times. Right, as
Don Carlos, 1982-83
season, Barcelona.

Two of my four
debuts in 1983:
above, as Romeo in
Romeo et Juliette,
Barcelona; right, as
Calaf in *Turandot*,
Vienna. Though
I had opening night
jitters, this
performance turned
out to be a great
success and was
recorded live
by CBS.

My other two role debuts in 1983 were Manrico in *Il trovatore*, London, (not pictured) and Jean (right) in *Herodiade*, Barcelona.

With Mirella Freni, one of my favourite colleagues, at a Christmas benefit concert for a hospital in Ravenna.

In the title role of *Andrea Chenier*, Royal Opera House, London, 1984.

The make-up artist works on my very first Canio, in *I pagliacci*, Madrid, 1986. Unique interaction with Ilona Tokody's Nedda intensified my portrayal of the aging clown. That same year I tried my hand at film acting: right, as the legendary tenor Julian Gayarre in the film Final Romance.

In the title role of *Werther*, with Agnes Baltsa as Charlotte, Vienna Staatsoper, 1986.

dollars. Then it gets a ruthless review in the most important newspapers. What happens? It's a flop and closes because the American public does not or will not try to form its own opinion.

Some critics are venerated like gods, and not surprisingly, they see themselves as the high priests of culture. Whatever falls short of their standards is automatically thrust into oblivion. Fortunately, reviews, good or bad, lose their weight when an artist has reached a certain professional level and gained the unconditional support of many fans and friends. I certainly enjoy praise, but it's not vitally important any more.

It's amusing today to read the tons of ecstatic words lavished on the incomparable Maria Callas. Reviewers trip over their own phrases for the opportunity to rehash yet another outdated eulogy. At the same time, I recall how often she was torn apart, professionally and artistically, by these same people. During her lifetime, Callas was almost destroyed by the critics.

Whom should we believe? It doesn't always take years of historical perspective to be surprised by the differences in critical opinion. Just skim through two different newspapers on the same day. Read the comments, and you will wonder if these people actually attended the same performance!

I remember the first time I was truly happy about a negative review. It was after singing *Carmen* at the Metropolitan Opera. Among other things, the reviewer said that I had not only the good but also the bad qualities of Giuseppe Di Stefano. On the same day another critic claimed my performance to be my best acting in New York! Again, this discrepancy. So who is right? I would've lost my sanity a long time ago if I took seriously everything that was written about me.

I believe in the public. What really counts is their response to my art. It doesn't matter if the audience consists
of 2,000 people in an opera house or of millions in front of
the television set. They make up their own minds to love my
voice or to reject it. I'm either a good singer whose art they
find inspiring or someone they can't warm up to at all. This
decision has always been in their hands, and I see no reason
that it should change. In the end, it's the public who decides
who and what will prevail on the stage.

We can well laugh at certain critical comments in the
past, for there have been some monumental misjudge-
ments. A Viennese critic, Eduard Hanslick, was caricatur-
ized by Wagner in *Die Meistersinger von Nurnberg* as the pe-
dantic Beckmesser, who forever picks on the tenor and his
song. Several modern reviewers have a similar tendency.
What's more, everybody's a critic! Even the composers
themselves perpetrated some very remarkable opinions in
their writings.

For example, Richard Strauss described *Aida* as "Indian music" and judged *Tosca* to be "pretentiousness of the
worst kind." Puccini retaliated by downgrading *Elektra* to
nothing more than a series of logarithms. Bizet
condemned *Un ballo in maschera* as "nauseating." Verdi
found *Lohengrin* insipid and "simply boring" while Wagner dubbed Franz Schubert a "third rate talent." Not even
Mozart was spared the mockery of his contemporaries. In a
few words, composer Giuseppe Sarti dismissed him and
his work. Mozart was "A barbarian without an ear who has
the audacity to write music!"

21

The Crisis in Opera

In the last few years, much has been said about certain serious problems lumped together as a so-called crisis in opera. This catchy phrasing refers primarily to the various financial difficulties that beset our institution. The escalating costs skyrocket while economic circumstances grow more stringent.

Nevertheless, when I hear this talk I think first of talent rather than purse strings. For me the upcoming generations of singers are the crux of the dilemma in our profession. I realize the subject is not new. The same complaints have been heard repeatedly for years, but I happen to believe that today, more than ever before, there is a desperate lack of true singing talent, a paucity that has reached frightening proportions.

Just a glance at the situation will show us that the appearances of success are deceiving. Our institution can be likened to an imposing pyramid. At its tip shine the current stars, big name operatic personalities. But they are not enough to assure a solid future. The foundation of this operatic pyramid must be renovated by gifted young singers who will be the building blocks at the base and in time will support the entire operatic structure. Without them, op-

era will collapse. The great singers will be gone, and there
will be no fresh, new replacements to take their place. If
only mediocre talents or performers with less than average
ability are left to carry on the great tradition who will even
want to buy a ticket? If the present trends continue among
the new generations of singers we will have more than just a
crisis on our hands, we may see the end of opera altogether.

In the history of opera, there have always existed elite
singers, those blessed with outstanding talents and voices.
They are a small group, but have always been the main reason that thousands of spectators flock to the great opera
houses. We all know that music lovers didn't go just to see
Tosca, they went to hear Callas. Today's situation is exactly
the same; only the names are different.

Of course, those who really love opera go to the theatre
also for the sake of the work itself, and they don't consider
it essential that the cast be headed by singing icons although I'm sure they wouldn't mind them. But serious
opera fans do demand singers who will at least show an average ability and are musically well-versed. They expect singers who are able to handle almost any problem and who can
correctly sing any role. These are basic necessities for that
sector of the public who are the mainstay and support of
our art form, the true pillars of opera. If these good people
decided to stay I home rather than be insulted by shoddy
opera performances we would be in serious trouble.

Furthermore, when opera theatres cannot offer well
sung, attractive productions, the new generation of audiences will not attend. Fortunately, the fascination with an
evening in the theatre is so powerful that many opera-goers
overlook certain faults in a production, preferring to see a
live performance rather than only listen to a recording, no
matter how perfect, or watch a video tape. But the first task

on our agenda is to induce new audiences to come to the theatre.

Again, it is the name singers who have the greatest promotional value, the box office draw, as it were, because they are the ones who are the most familiar through constant media exposure. Yet despite the selling power of these stars, many lesser opera directors can't afford them and are forced to drop the so-called *stagione* system in which famous guest singers appear seasonally in their small theatres. Instead, the directors find that they must adopt the more economical repertory system whereby operas are mounted entirely by the resident company.

Once in a while, however, under the guidance of a creative director, a few small theatres experience a boomerang effect, somehow raising the funds required to pay the top fees demanded by stars. Even though this is hard to imagine I personally know of instances in which a small, rather unknown house is suddenly able to pay the same, if not higher, salaries as the most prestigious theatres in the world. These individual directors may be motivated by vanity in their fund-raising solution to the crisis in opera.

Overleaf.
Working outside the pale of opera: as Julian Gayarre, with Sydne Rome, in the film, *Final romance.*

22

Between Performances

Please don't think that a well-known opera singer has much time for himself. My life is given over to a career whose demands pull in all directions. The performances, rehearsals, recording dates, hours of study, receptions I can't miss, and other duties seem endless. Barely a few slim moments, a rather narrow margin of my existence, can be saved for hobbies and leisure. Nevertheless, mine is a many-sided profession filled with certain rewards.

For one thing, it offers me chances to meet some of the world's most interesting people. (I must say that by "interesting people" I don't mean the international jet set. On the whole, these darlings of the tabloids strike me as sterile and boring. Of course, I've met a few sensible and charming jet setters, but they were exceptions.) A truly engrossing person is someone like the President of Yale University. I met him at a banquet in New York where we chatted for an hour and a half. I found myself transported into another world. Even though I felt somewhat dwarfed by this intellectual giant, our conversation opened new vistas to me and was truly an occasion of personal growth.

Among my non-musical interests I follow the ups and downs of politics, but strictly as a ring-side observer. I have no interest in trying to shape political events or policies, and given my position it would be questionable for me to make public political statements. Since I'm well-known and possibly even a role model in some circles, especially among my own people, I know that anything I might say would carry a good deal of weight. I will not abuse this power. I've always been suspicious of artists who use their popularity to advance some pet ideology. They generally know as much, or as little about politics as any other average citizen, so their opinions shouldn't be used to sway people. For the same reason, singers shouldn't allow themselves to be exploited by politicians who care only about one thing, to be elected to office.

My vote goes to those political leaders who command my respect, and that happens only when they are men who champion freedom, oppose tyranny, and use their power to uphold justice. I take my hat off to the statesmen who are unafraid of dealing with the vital issues of our times, men gifted with a future vision well beyond the scope of the average citizen.

Yet I have an equal admiration for others who are not leaders of men at all, the anonymous heroes who forge ahead through the hardships of each day, and the scientists who seek new horizons in all branches of knowledge. Concerning the latter I must say that lately I had good reasons to make special room in my heart for the men and women who labour in the medical sciences.

Some of the most intriguing people, however, are found in my own world of opera. I've met various outstanding personalities during my career and want to assure you that when we opera professionals meet we don't just talk about music and singing.

Much as I love music, I could never concentrate only on my work and miss the enjoyment derived from the other fine arts. They are basic necessities in my life. For instance, I've always had strong ties with painting. When we were children our parents instilled in us a deep pride for the artistic richness of Spain, a land of painters. Whenever I got hold of one of those oversized art books, I buried myself in its colour plates and sketches. I wanted to know all about the artists who had created such wonders and read everything I could about their lives and works. As a family, we visited museums and galleries, seeking out every exhibit that came our way.

Unfortunately I could not explore the Prado until I was older. The collection in Madrid's famous museum includes some of the greatest art in the world and I remember the impact of my first visit there. I marvelled as I walked the galleries of this legendary building, overwhelmed by roomfuls and roomfuls of masterpieces. I recognized works by such geniuses as El Greco, Titian, Rubens and, of course, Spain's own Velasquez and Goya. Seeing them in all their original glory was breathtaking, a privilege and a boon.

The great painters, sculptors, and architects of history have my unqualified admiration. El Greco enthrals me, and I find intriguing the work of our Catalan masters, Salvador Dali and Joan Miró.

My emotions are roused by the monumental works of Michelangelo, and I am enthused by the architectural designs of the great Palladio. But there is one master artist whom I prefer above all others. In contrast to my other favourite painters, who come from southern countries, he is the product of a northern culture. I mean that genius who was Rembrandt; there's such greatness in his work that I could contemplate it forever. In fact I'm so attuned

to his style that I love paintings which are no more than attributed to him.

Though art gives me much pleasure, literature is one
of my greatest passions. I've always been a reader, and
books are my companions wherever I go. The truth is that
sometimes I love reading as much as I love music. The type
of book I choose depends on my state of mind. From the
great classics to novels by Harold Robbins, there's a wide
range for selection, and I can truthfully say I am interested in almost every kind of writing.

It's not easy for me to name my all-time favourite au-
thors, but two Spanish poets are at the top of my list, Antonio Machado and Pedro Salinas, whose work I've recently
come to know more deeply. His cycle of lyrical poems
titled *La voz a ti debida* is so compelling that I'm planning
to record it as songs. I've already found the right composer for this album in Antonio Parera, another compa-
triot of mine.

As for my favourite books, I can definitely name one,
The Gardener, by Rabindranath Tagore. It's a small volume, regarded by many as dated and overly lofty, but I
have read and reread it countless times. Though out of
fashion today, the Hindu author has always inspired me
with his poems of love and life. When I was unhappy, out of
sorts with myself, or depressed, I found courage and
strength in Tagore's pages. He showed me how to look at
life, and the rich poetry of his language, considered too
full of pathos by some, struck a deep chord in me. I used to
carry it with me as though it were some sort of personal
Bible. And even though I had my family and my friends to
talk with, when I needed support *The Gardener* was always
my first refuge. Reading is a great diversion for me. Often
I have several books working at the same time and choose

them according to my mood.

Something similar happens with music. For example, can you imagine someone who listens only to Mahler, without interruption? Such a person would have to be either mad or little short of a fanatic. It's popularly believed that professional musicians who have been trained in classical music don't care about any other types of composition. I can assure you that in my case it's totally untrue. I respect every form of music, as long as it's good music.

For example let's take the music of the Beatles. When they first leaped into fame, I was totally absorbed in my own studies. I had no time to explore their music, and for me, they were just another pop group. It was only much later that I discovered and learned to treasure the extraordinary qualities of their compositions and lyrics. Today I'm beginning to realize their true worth as some of their songs are among the most beautiful I know and are practically modern classics in their own right.

Sooner or later in discussing popular music, we opera singers have to face the usual question: why don't we sing these songs? Along with the works of Verdi, Puccini, and Bizet, why not make a recording or two of popular music or even give a recital of pop songs? How marvellous it would be, an exciting renewal! Besides, it's nothing new, tenors have wandered into unknown territories before. Caruso, Gigli, Schipa and a string of other singers took advantage of their position as influential stars and sang pop tunes as well as classic music. Some of my colleagues make a point of sounding like opera tenors, no matter how simple the song. Others, however, abandon the grand manner and choose to adapt their interpretation to the tune, as Giuseppe di Stefano did when singing delightfully Neapolitan songs.

My own venture into the realm of popular music was a happy one in several respects. Working with some of the greatest talents in the music industry, I collaborated in recording two of America's most famous musicals, *South Pacific* and *West Side story*. In the last twenty years, the latter had achieved a great success on Broadway and was made into an Oscar-winning film. I consider it a work of exceptional appeal and charm. Recording it was like being part of history, since it was the occasion for Leonard Bernstein, its composer, to conduct it for the first time. His presence alone made this project an extraordinary happening.

My reasons for singing the so-called popular music are several. First, I enjoy it, as do millions of other fans. I also find it relaxing to sing. But deep down I confess to an ulterior motive: I sing popular tunes because I believe that this is the way to capture new fans for the opera. My hope is that record buyers who listen to *South Pacific* and *West Side story* may develop an interest in Carreras the vocalist and then discover through him a whole new world of beauty and fascination—the opera.

2 3

The Acoustical Wars

THE FIRST time a tenor, or any singer, walks onto the stage of an unfamiliar theatre, he must check out two important but capricious factors, the standard pitch of the orchestra and the acoustical peculiarities of the building.

Strangely, what is known as "standard" pitch is not really standard at all. In fact, the standard A pitch has been argued about for at least a century, being raised so often it's reached the point where it makes a tenor's life very difficult. The slight difference in pitch is barely noticeable to the average listener; at best he'll only enjoy the bright sound of the orchestra since, at this higher frequency, the notes made by modern orchestral instruments have a greater brilliance. But for the singer to have to "tune higher" is much more of a physical struggle than in the time of Caruso or Gigli, who didn't have to sing as high as a tenor today to reach a B-flat. No wonder transposing is a must. I've found that the standard pitch used by orchestras in central Europe is higher than in Britain or America.

The development of standard pitch makes an interesting story, with a few curious twists. In 1885, musical experts around the world met in Vienna at the International

Conference on Standard Pitch. Everyone agreed to set the standard A pitch at 435 vibrations per second. But in no time at all, individual orchestras, especially those working in larger concert halls and theatres, turned a deaf ear to this decision and, in order to be heard better, set about raising their pitch. Each orchestra had its own standard, one that suited its own particular acoustical space. More intensity and more orchestral brilliance were the goals.

News travelled through the opera grapevine that a singer could negotiate the standard pitch with certain orchestras and, naturally, the star had more clout than other performers. Some opera greats even maneuvered to have the pitch set lower than 435 vibrations per second just to protect their voices. For a while, the Vienna Court Opera used more than six tuning forks, ranging from 434 to 445 vibrations per second, and it all depended on the bias, the mood, or the ability of the singer as to which one was used.

Officially, in the 1930s, the universal standard pitch was raised to 440 vibrations per second, a rule which is still on the books today. But once again, individual orchestras decided to push their own pitch still higher—as high as 450 vibrations per second. Whenever musicians and singers get together, the debate goes on, as it always has in the past. The public became aware of this technical turmoil in 1988, when two Italian senators warned that the tendency to keep raising the pitch should be stopped and the whole matter should be legally settled once and for all. They favoured setting the pitch at 432 vibrations per second (432 Hertz) as an ideal frequency for the human voice. Giuseppe Verdi himself had once proposed this standard pitch, and law to this effect had already been passed by the Italian government in 1884. These two senators lobbied for a more "human" standard pitch, maintaining that we were losing good singers, especially in opera, because of the demand for

such a high vocal range and extravagant volume. They argued that new talent was being forced out. Now, I wouldn't
defend the case for a lower standard pitch so dramatically,
but I certainly wouldn't mind dropping closer to the historic standard pitch of 435 Hertz, just to be free of unneces-
sary worry and bother.

On the subject of acoustics, I have come across marked
differences in theatres. To us singers, what matters most is
that the sound of our voice, once we send it out, comes back
to us, but not too strongly. I must be able to hear myself. It's
horrendously difficult to sing if the sound doesn't bounce
back. Nothing can make you feel more insecure! How else
can you judge if the volume is right, if the resonance is rich
enough, and so on? I have found the acoustics in the old
opera houses to be much better than the acoustics in our
modern auditoriums. Perhaps the difference is in the
building materials since, in my experience, the size of the
structure doesn't make any difference. To sing in a smaller
auditorium is not necessarily better. I know small theatres
with acoustics that can't begin to match the phenomenal
acoustics of the cavernous Scala in Milan.

Which brings us to another kind of acoustical war. At
La Scala, there is one special spot on the stage where your
voice is sure to resonate with greater sharpness, intensity,
and volume. Every singer covets this spot, and some refuse
to budge from it. I've never witnessed an on-stage fight, but
I know old stories about singers, especially formidable
prima donnas, whose violent refusals to give up their
acoustical advantage are part of this theatre's legendary
past. Undeniably, strange acoustical experiences do occur
at La Scala. If you happen to be singing while you're crossing the stage, as you pass over this famous spot, it sounds as
if someone quickly turned an amplifier on and off. On the
stage of the Vienna Staatsoper, there's a similar phenome-

non although the jump in volume between the mystery spot and the rest of the stage is minimal. The zone where the acoustics are better is larger at the Staatsoper than at La Scala, but not nearly as impressive.

Whatever the theatre, the smart singer must always ask himself, "Where is the best place to stand on the stage so that the acoustics will work for me?" It's usually a mistake to think you'll be heard better if you stand down stage, although it's a possibility. Each theatre and each stage is different. Even the set design can have a telling effect on acoustics, and what's acoustically true for one opera set may be different in the next.

For instance, if the set is designed to enclose the stage, the result is a shell effect. This type of design actually helps magnify the sound, and the singer finds it easy to project his voice. If the set is open at the back, the singer has to work harder to be heard. Also, the materials chosen by the designer to create the decor and the props affect the acoustics. Fabrics especially can deaden the sound. Carpets are the worst; they literally soak it up. The designers tell us it's our imagination, that we're just hysterical types. Not true. We've never seen eye to eye with designers over the effect of scrims, those barely visible net curtains sometimes dropped between us on stage and the orchestra. Scrims may not change the intensity of the sound very much, but they play havoc with the harmony and rapport between the singer and the musicians. Anyone who claims this isn't true obviously never sang on stage or worked in the orchestra.

In spite of all these preferences and prejudices about what helps or hurts the acoustics, the decisive factor is the theatre building itself. If someone asked me which houses have the best acoustics I'd list them in the following order: La Scala in Milan, Vienna Staatsoper, Liceo in Barcelona, Teatro Colon in Buenos Aires, Nationaltheater of Munich and Teatro San Carlo in Naples. I hear the Festspielhaus in Bayreuth, designed by Richard Wagner himself, has phenomenal acoustics; unfortunately, I've yet to perform there.

Perhaps I should stop here and say something about Bayreuth and Wagner. The relatively lighter voices of opera singers from Southern Europe make Wagner's Festspielhaus virtually a forbidden territory for them. They're not loud enough or trained to tread that stage. In my case, I don't think this will change soon. As attracted as I am to the possibility of appearing in one of the operas composed by this genius, the language barrier is a big headache. I think a person should be able to speak a language fluently before trying to sing opera in it. To painstakingly learn the words by rote, syllable by syllable, is not my cup of tea. I'm the type who has to know exactly what I'm saying at any given moment while I sing. Thus the language of Richard Wagner is almost an insurmountable obstacle course for me. A wrong accent, an incorrect emphasis, a strange inflection, these little mistakes can sabotage even the most beautiful note or the best-sung phrase. Since I place very high demands on myself I'm afraid the opera world will have to wait a very long time for my Wagnerian debut.

One evening, during the already legendary first run of *Don Carlos* conducted by Herbert von Karajan, I was having dinner at a restaurant with some friends. Feeling relaxed and creative, we began to fantasize about a daring Wagnerian project. It was our opinion that everyone in the *Don Carlos* cast could sing a role in *Lohengrin,* provided it was in Italian, of course, and perhaps first as a recording. We'd cast Mirella Freni as Elsa, Fiorenza Cossotto as Ortrud, Nicolai Ghiaurov as the king, Piero Cappuccilli as Telramund, and myself as Lohengrin. It was an intriguing idea, but one of pure fantasy!

Sara Giordano, widow of composer Umberto Giordano, honoured me with a visit after the opening of *Andrea Chenier* at La Scala in 1982.

24

Artist Versus Man

SPLENDOUR, FAME, luxury, and wealth, those are the things the public imagines in the life of a tenor who is coveted and cosseted by all the opera houses of the world. That we work hard for these trappings of fame, that we strive within ourselves continuously to achieve such eminence is something they generally don't realize. The very demand for our services is what forces us to live like gypsies, trekking endlessly around the world. Our life isn't nearly as much fun as it seems, and it can even cause us great harm by separating us from our loved ones. No, I'm not complaining about our lifestyle, and much less lamenting my own fate! I always wanted to sing, and, after all the years of hard work, my professional dreams came true.

What more can I ask of life? Well, frankly, there are moments when I get fed up with packing and unpacking suitcases. I'm also tired of being alone so often. Strange, isn't it, that a tenor who's usually besieged by admiring fans and always surrounded by people can still feel very much alone. This loneliness grows until it becomes a problem you only discover after you've attained a certain level of success and are finally established. Yes, the situation had me worried a long time before my illness; I wondered if the life of a singer wasn't somewhat unhinged or mad by any standard.

At the beginning of my career, everything was new and I lived in constant fascination. I was caught up in my own enthusiasm, ecstatic over the realization of my dreams, and ready to take on any challenge to further my career. If asked, I would have given a concert in the train while travelling from an engagement in Paris to one in Milan. I would have flown on a day's notice to Tokyo to make a recording, learned a new score on the return flight, and never grumbled. Work was my obsession in those early years. I didn't want to miss one chance to perform with such and such conductor and this or that colleague. There were countless recordings and appearances, endless trips from concert halls to important opera houses.

I think that every artist follows the same path and ends by taking on more than he can manage. It's not surprising because when all your dreams of a singing career finally come true, when you feel that you have arrived after so much struggle, you don't want to pass up even the smallest tidbit. Would you fail to jump aboard the glory train when it might never pass your way again?

I did everything with pleasure and discipline, giving it my all. The great number of offers that poured in made me very happy. If it were physically and technically possible, I'd have performed somewhere every evening of the year.

But one day I stopped. Having practically reached the top of the opera world, I looked around. And I saw Carreras the man suffering in the shadow of Carreras the artist. Carreras the man began to say, "Well and good! As an artist, you've reached an extremely comfortable place. You've participated in fabulous projects. You're in a splendid position! But what happened to *me*?" And he begged the artist, "Give me a little of this life, too. I don't see why I must exist for weeks, going from one hotel room to another. Why must I be separated from my family? Why must I constantly worry about my voice? I don't understand! How I envy normal people who sit for eleven months in an office and then take a month long vacation."

But no matter what the voice said, I had to admit in all honesty that Carreras the artist is a privileged fellow who does whatever he likes and who sees all his wishes fulfilled. He's a success and probably ninety-nine percent of the public would gladly exchange places with him any time. There's a split within my soul, a double personality, and the successful artist is the stronger. He holds the man down, forcing his will upon him until the man ultimately accepts his fate.

Yet I was not at ease and my soul-searching dialogue was far from over; I kept it up until it became the basis of my present, rather different view of life.

There's a voice of reason within me that clashes with my temperament. For example when I have to solve a problem or have an idea knocking about in my head, I just can't sit quietly at home, watching television. I'm simply not like others who can forget or push aside their tasks. They can say to themselves, "Tomorrow, at the office, I'll do what I have to do" and relax, play tennis, or go for a swim. Their motto, "Everything in its own time," certainly sounds like the right attitude towards life. The only hitch is that one has to learn to live by such a philosophy. And I can't.

Let me try to describe my personality. I can only sit down and be still when I have a book in my hand. I can't make myself concentrate on television, even for half an hour, unless there's a football match on. Otherwise, I always have to make a phone call or do something else as well. If I'm not busy for two days in a row, I don't know what to do with myself. For this reason, I've never been able to take a vacation in the usual sense of the word. It's inconceivable for me to lie quietly in the sun even for fifteen minutes. I'd get bored and overheated. (Actually, I think that most vacationers feel as I do, but they work on a suntan out of vanity.)

No, for me a two week vacation in the Bahamas isn't the ideal rest. That's not my style. But I know what I like. When I happen to be at home in Spain, meeting my closest friends, enjoying a good conversation, playing cards, and generally being at ease, that to me is relaxation.

For a long time, however, I've been dreaming about a very special vacation, which hopefully I'll be able to take one day. With three friends in a camper, I'd roam all over the United States, my only necessities of life being jeans, a toothbrush, and a credit card. No need to worry about flights, engagements, tuxedos, tails. No need to be constantly aware of my voice. This is a dream I've cherished for years, more a chance for adventure than for vacation.

But first I want to take care of another, more pressing business, and that is to get to know Spain better. There's a certain irony in that we travel to the ends of the earth, but know little or nothing about what's next door to us. I think a little of this happens to everybody. After my illness, I vowed to explore our province of Andalusia. Naturally, the cities of this fabled land—Granada, Seville, Malaga, Cordoba—are well known to me already, but I never found time to explore the countryside. There are tiny villages and picturesque spots in such blissful seclusion that they have yet to be charted. Undoubtedly, Andalusia is one of the most beautiful places on earth, and it's a shame for a Spaniard like myself to know her only superficially.

Speaking of a holiday for a singer, it's a problem that has been subject to public discussion. In recent years, the critics were quick to voice their disapproval whenever a tenor had an off night. The shouts would begin, "No wonder! They all sing too much and too often. Not one of them wants to take off even for a two-week vacation!" This is absolutely silly, at least where I am concerned. My golden rule has always been to sing two or three performances a week and have a minimum two days of rest between them. It's a practice that lets me have the necessary time to recuperate and to get back in the mood to sing. If the break stretches for a longer time, say for a week, I begin to miss singing so much that my state of mind quickly hits rock bottom. For someone whose nature compels him to sing, singing is not harmful, as long as the instrument is in good condition. Besides, long rests are not good for the voice either.

There are exceptions to my golden rule, but they aren't planned or anticipated. I remember an instance when I received an afternoon call from the management of La Scala in Milan. They asked me if I would substitute for Pavarotti, unexpectedly indisposed, in *Un ballo in maschera* that very same night. I complied gladly with their request though my own schedule was full. I had sung *La Bohème* in Nice the previous night and was scheduled for *Don Carlos* at La Scala the following day. Undoubtedly it was a strain to sing three days in a row, but, thankfully, I succeeded without special problems.

Someone once showed me a pages long list with the appearances of the legendary tenor, Helge Rosvaenge. The number of his performances was as incredible as the roles in his repertoire. In October of 1936, for example, he sang almost daily in several European cities. He crossed and recrossed the continent. There were an incredible 16 opera performances and 9 concerts. One after another, he sang the following operas: *La Bohème, Rigoletto, Un ballo in maschera, Madama Butterfly, Zauberflote, Il trovatore, Aida, La traviata,* and *Carmen.* An enormous accomplishment, to say the least! How he managed all these performances is beyond me. You have to remember that leaping from one opera house to the other was not a simple feat in the thirties. Travelling then was neither speedy nor comfortable. As I scan Rosvaenge's list, I can only smile at those who complain that today's opera singers are doing far too much singing.

25

What Price a Singer?

"Why is opera so expensive?" Everybody wants to know, and right away one answer is heard above the rest: "Because the stars' salaries are so high!" This sounds good, and it's definitely an easy sell to the public, but it's not true.

Those familiar with the opera world know that the enormous financial investments in opera are diverted before they reach the opera singers. There are many other expenses to consider: the great collective orchestra, the chorus, technicians, and, naturally, the costs incurred by management.

Thus well over seventy-five percent of the ticket price is disposed of long before the first singer sets foot on stage. With each passing season, theatre costs rise in an unparalleled fashion, and the financial margin for artistic production gets narrower and narrower. Recent statistics indicate that the share of a theatre's funds allotted for the soloists' salaries continues in only one direction, downhill. It's possible that, on the whole, the fees for the singers are too high, but we have to consider that the cost of these "divos" is governed by a distinct set of rules. Even if their salaries seem preposterous an opera house that has the means to pay them will be compensated by matching box office returns. After all, the more popular the cast, the more tickets are sold and the greater financial benefits for the house. This advantage is observed repeatedly and is the rule, not the exception, in all the important opera theatres of the world.

To discuss salaries and figures is always a delicate matter, and naturally we don't need to justify ourselves. But I'd like at least to point out a few pertinent facts. To do this, I must backtrack and digress for a moment.

There are a number of intellectual professions that carry tremendous responsibility. For example, let's examine the case of the surgeon whose abilities prove the difference between life and death for a patient. A singer is no match for this analogy. Does it really matter if a tenor misses a high C? No. The next day he sings somewhere else, and the mishap is forgotten. But then we come to psychological pressures, and that's another matter altogether. As far as stress is concerned, you can realistically compare the tensions of performing an open heart surgery with singing in a premiere at La Scala.

On the other hand, a surgeon's responsibility is obviously a hundred, no, a thousand times greater than a singer's. I won't deny that a surgeon must be gifted by nature with a special ability. But relatively quite a number of people become first-rate surgeons; only a few singers reach the pinnacle of opera. By way of another analogy, an architect or a doctor has a long and hard road to travel before he can practice his profession. His eventual success represents years of difficult studies and work. The same is true of a singer. The crucial difference is that the singer must be endowed by nature with an exceptional voice. It's like tennis. Millions of people all over the world play the game, but only a few become top seed. Without talent, even the most exhaustive training will not make an Ivan Lendl or Boris Becker.

Talent and the right voice are gifts from God, and we are privileged by this divine favour. If enough will-power, discipline, intelligence and luck are added, you can become one of the few who actually fulfils the certain longings of millions of people. And as part of this group, you'll learn first-hand about the law of demand and supply. Since the demand for great singers far outweighs the supply it becomes obvious why theatre managers pay them such high salaries. In all honesty, I have to say that I'm glad things work out this way. Would anyone willingly say to the management, "No, don't pay me so much! I don't want money." It would be ridiculous and hypocritical to presume such readiness. Yet even if financial arrangements in the opera world were other than they are, I'd still work in an opera company as an employee with a fixed monthly income rather than choose another profession.

My great boon is that I'm not just doing something that gives me normal satisfaction, but something that I love with all my heart, something I firmly believe I was born to do. How lucky for me that, on top of all this, my profession lets me lead a pleasant, comfortable life to boot. Although certain fellow singers complain how difficult, strenuous, and complicated their life is, I maintain that it's really a magnificent way to live as long as you believe in what you're doing. I know that I won't change my mind no matter what difficulties might come my way. I can't imagine doing anything with my life other than singing, in spite of the problems and the stress.

Opera singers and sports champions feel the same psychological tensions. There are studies which show that a singer's pulse rate increases by fifty beats a minute as soon as he enters the stage. Just before and during an aria, peak rates were measured at up to two hundred pulse beats, considerably more than in any other performing artist. Perhaps the explanation is that mistakes by an actor, pianist, or other instrumental soloist have a less dramatic effect on the success of a production than a wrong note from a singer.

Any performer who says he is free of stage fright is not telling the truth. The tension is particularly dreadful before an important premiere . . . and every premiere is important. I had more than my share of opening night jitters before my first *Turandot* in Vienna. If a fairy godmother had flown into my dressing room and promised me, "Eat a hundred kilos of soap at once and you'll be tall as Franco Corelli tonight," I would've done it. Incidentally, this performance, led by Lorin Maazel, with Eva Marton and Katia Ricciarelli, became for all of us a resounding triumph.

On the day of a performance, my feelings of stress begin in the morning. As a singer, I can't depend entirely on talent and skill. These are only basic elements that can come to naught without nature's help. The slightest little twinge causes problems. Given that everything is going well physically, you still can't escape the psychological tension. It's always there, a threat even if you've sung the role a hundred times.

Doubts and uncertainties go through your mind. People expect a certain performance from you, they know how you've done this particular aria before, and they know how you usually act this or that part. You've got to be at least as good as that other time. I've developed a habit that helps me relax. I arrive at the theatre long before curtain time. And I welcome the distraction when friends and colleagues drop by my dressing room to chat for a moment. Just knowing I'm in my opera environment is enough to ease much of my tension.

As hysterical as some singers are before a performance, others are just as stoic. Once I was at a party with Alfredo Kraus when shortly before seven he turned to me and said, "Well, I've got to go. My performance starts at eight." Alfredo was singing in *The daughter of the regiment,* and usually a tenor barricades himself for days before singing such a demanding score.

On another occasion we were doing a run of *Aida* at Salzburg, and as curtain time drew near my friend Piero Cappuccilli came to my dressing room to inquire how I was feeling. "Wonderful!" I told him. "If only this damn difficult aria wasn't right at the beginning." But, according to Piero, this was not a problem, and to show me he proceeded to sing the last part of "Celeste Aida", including the feared B-flat at the end. He didn't want to undermine my courage. On the contrary. His demonstration was meant to calm my nerves. "If I can do this as a baritone," he affirmed, "you as a tenor can surely do it much better!"

I have to repeat, despite these bad sides, our profession is one of the most wonderful anyone can choose even if we can't practice it our entire lives. Singing usually has a limited life span. You spend ten years scrambling to get to the top, then you have ten good years, and then everything is over. Naturally, during the working years, everyone tries to earn as much as possible.

In my career, I had great luck, it took me only three years to reach my goal, and I've performed in all the major cities of the world, with corresponding growth in salaries. Of course, those outside our profession don't realize that we have to spend enormous sums. Our incomes are practically devoured by travel, hotels, and a necessary lifestyle. Today, when it comes to finances I'm doing very well. I can go to a car dealership and, looking through the showroom, announce, "I like that car back there against the wall. I'll

A happy moment during the rehearsal for the Three Tenors Concert, July 1990. Around me: Placido Domingo, our conductor, Zubin Mehta, and Luciano Pavarotti.

take it with me." Then I pay and drive off. But, although I'm probably regarded as one of the best paid tenors in the world, I'm not a millionaire, though once I pretended to be. It was in Paris, and I needed a taxi to go from my hotel to an important meeting. After waiting an eternity, I managed to stop one. When I gave the cabbie the address, he calmly answered, "Better take the Metro, it's faster." And he opened the car door, indicating that I should get out. I was furious because the Metro station was quite a distance away! So with great dignity I told the taxi driver, "I'm a millionaire, and millionaires don't take the Metro." Whereupon he and I sped off, and I could see he hoped for a tip, commensurate with my new-found economic status.

26

Favourite Operas

"WHICH OPERA would you take with you if you knew you were to be shipwrecked on a desert island?" I am often asked this classic question.

If I were to be marooned for a long time, I certainly wouldn't or couldn't limit myself to either one composer or one opera. I would bring with me at least one work by each of the great masters—recorded by singers that would be my ideal casts.

Mozart would probably be my first choice, but I would flip a coin to decide whether to bring *The marriage of Figaro* or *Don Giovanni*. From Rossini, the selection is clear, *The barber of Seville*. At one time there were plans to record this opera with Claudio Abbado as conductor and a surprise cast of Domingo as Figaro and, myself, as Count Almaviva. But, in the end this project was not realized.

Continuing to gather together my island collection, I would take Bellini's *Norma* and, depending on my mood at the time, Donizetti's humorous *L'elisir d'amore* or the dramatic *Roberto Devereux*. I would bring along *Tristan und Isolde* by Wagner and also throw in the last rousing twenty minutes from the first act of *Die Walkure*. From Bizet, there is but one choice, *Carmen*. From Puccini, *La Bohème* or

Manon Lescaut. And from Richard Strauss, I would want *Der Rosenkavalier.*

From Verdi? To choose just one of Verdi's operas would be difficult. *La traviata, Rigoletto, Il trovatore,* and *Un ballo in maschera,* each one of these is a masterpiece that I would love to have on that proverbial island.

Un ballo is undeniably etched in my memory. I sang my very first Riccardo in Parma, a city steeped in opera. And the very next day, I made my debut as a father: my son Alberto was born! Five years later, I was recording *Ballo* in London, and we happened to finish one day earlier than expected; I flew back to Spain and arrived home on exactly the same day that my daughter Julia was born. So in my mind *Ballo* is always fondly remembered and entwined with two of the most important events in my personal life.

Ballo is also special to me for another reason, a reason more professional than personal. It was in *Ballo* that I made my debut at La Scala, a pinnacle in an opera singer's career.

Yet if I had to choose only one Verdi opera, it would not be *Ballo.* After painful deliberations, I would leave behind all of the masterpieces I mentioned earlier. Instead, I would bring his Spanish prince to my island. I would choose *Don Carlos* to keep me company. But enough of this fantasy.

Allow me the luxury of changing the island question slightly. I would like to take the opportunity to focus not on the operas, but on the roles that I love the most, the two roles that are most often associated with me. Of all the characters I've played, I must admit that the creative Rodolfo in Puccini's *La Bohème* and the destructive Don José in Bizet's *Carmen* are my favourites. I say this even though these two roles are intrinsically very different, both in their vocal requirements and in what they require by way of dramatic interpretation.

Even as a student, I was fascinated by the story-line of *La Bohème*. Its theme appealed to me more than any other opera. I found it full of wonderful poetry, the poetry of everyday lives of Parisian artists. The attraction was not surprising. Students everywhere can identify with the starving yet joyful quartet of Parisian bohemians living in a garret; the painter, the musician, the philosopher, and the poet. The impassioned, mercurial poet Rodolfo . . . he was my man! Because I wanted to understand the opera better and gain more insight into the characters I went back to the literary source, Henri Murger's novel, *Scenes de la Vie de Bohème*. Murger, a 19th century journalist, himself was a fickle and colourful figure. He wanted to be a painter, but he earned his living writing. In his news stories, he portrayed the life of the artists and bohemians around him. These newspaper articles became the basis for his novel, and, within the socio-economic conditions of his time, Murger found fame and fortune.

I was captivated by Rodolfo's melancholy and by the irony that appears here and there throughout the story. Any man who could write so convincingly about artists and their surroundings must have, himself, lived such a life. His novel is more than a work of fiction, it's a picture of reality.

That Puccini was able to capture the atmosphere of Paris so faithfully in his music is a tribute to his genius. I find it incredible that he never even saw the city. His characterizations are superb. Rodolfo and his friends exist on the fringe of life. And Puccini's music expresses their poignant fate so well. It's this quality, this interpretation by the great composer, that impressed me from the very beginning, even when I was a student.

In its musical style, *La Bohème* is a work of extraordinary elegance. The dialogue between the singing voices and the orchestra is pure magic, regardless if you are listening to an intimate love duet or a brilliant ensemble. In the arias, every note conveys passion and devotion. His lyrics contain some of the most unforgettable passages in opera, yet the words are simple, the poetry uncomplicated. Rodolfo is a challenging role. I can think of no other work in which the tenor must express so many emotions: love, jealousy, misery, hope and, finally, despair.

For me, the third act of *La Bohème* is the most crucial dramatically and most demanding vocally. When Mimi and Rodolfo meet again it is one of the most tender scenes of operatic literature. Only the incomparable Herbert von Karajan conducted this scene with the intensity and brilliance worthy of Puccini. I remember that during a rehearsal in the Vienna Staatsoper, Karajan interrupted the third act during the mid-winter scene. In the midst of winter and falling snow, he began to shout accusingly at us, "You move as if you were in cold storage!" Mirella Freni, our Mimi, responded, "But, Maestro, what else are we supposed to do? We are cold! And besides, it *is* snowing!"

I love playing Rodolfo because he is a young man who invites affection and understanding. When the audience first meets him, he seems a little frivolous and immature. In the farewell scene of Act III, we see him growing wiser. He begins to show his fine and noble side. In the fourth act all that is good in him is finally revealed. I find it lucky that composers cast tenors as lovers and heroes. This is probably because tenors sound "younger" than baritones and basses. And when it comes to getting the sympathy of the audience, tenors always come out ahead. Then too, tenors seldom die on stage. It is remarkable how in Puccini's six great operas five of the tenors live. Only one, Cavaradossi, dies.

Speaking of Cavaradossi, my daughter Julia became the heroine of a theatre incident. She was only three years old when she came to see me in an opera for the first time. We were doing *Tosca* in Madrid. When Cavaradossi collapsed under the volley of the firing squad, little Julia became frightened and shouted for all to hear, "Why are those bad men killing my father?"

When studying a role, it is natural for a singer to look for parallels in his own character, to identify with the role. I can see myself in Rodolfo, the poet, but I can also identify with Don José, the soldier.

Without any doubt, the role of Don José in *Carmen* is the most important that I have undertaken so far. From 1982 through 1987, I sang this part more than a hundred times in Madrid, Milan, Salzburg, Vienna, London, New York, and Barcelona to mention just the most important places. The productions were as diverse as the men who staged them, Ponnelle, Zeffirelli, and Hall. And the musical directors have been as varied as the productions—maestros such as Karajan, Maazel, Levine and Abbado. My Carmen, however, has been played most often by one leading lady, the magnificent Agnes Baltsa.

I consider *Carmen* to be the most popular work of all time. If a street survey were taken and passersby were asked to name the first opera that comes to mind, nine out of ten people would say *Carmen*. I am convinced of this. Who cannot hum the Toreador Song? Who cannot recall the Habanera? The popularity of the bullfighter's tune is incredible. Yet, amazingly enough, this opera had a chequered beginning. Its premiere was greeted by the public with reserve and by the press with disdain. Poor Bizet died three months after its unfortunate premiere and never saw it develop into a great success.

Because *Carmen* is so well-known, the singer is under tremendous pressure. You can sense that the audience is singing along with you and you feel considerably more apprehensive than usual. It is as if you were being given a comparative test. The difficulty of any *spinto* role such as Don José lies in bringing together the lyrical and the dramatic. Act I demands a lyric interpretation; too strong a tenor will destroy the charm of the duet with Micaela. Act II requires power and dramatic flourish to pull off the Flower Song and its final B-flat.

At Salzburg, Karajan wanted me to sing this B-flat with a head-tone. The difficulty was that I had to sing it softly when tenors usually sing it loudly. Long discussions followed his requested change. There were certain things that could be done only with Karajan and by Karajan; for example, to sing this B-flat softly. Karajan's concept of this aria was uniquely individual, and he guided the orchestra accordingly, with appropriate dynamics. Under his hand, the aria became a declaration of love. He imbued it with unbelievable delicacy. His compelling interpretation of the Flower Song could end in no other way but pianissimo.

But many listeners do not understand Karajan's interpretation. When they hear the end they think, "Aha! This tenor cannot sing a B-flat with a chest-tone!" Today's audiences have come to expect great resounding high notes from the tenor, and to sing a B-flat pianissimo in La Scala is tantamount to professional suicide. Karajan was looking for a tenor who could not only sing the last note pianissimo, but a tenor who had the professional courage to do so. I did, and enjoyed crowning the aria with exactly the soft, evocative B-flat the Maestro wished. Later, when I reverted to the usual loud ending, I liked the bigger sound, too.

After the Flower Song, Don José undergoes another transformation. With the appearance of Lieutenant Zuniga, the tenor part must become more dramatic. Here the singer must emphasize the accents or be lost. The interpretive challenge in Act III is to marry the lyric to the dramatic, in spite of the particularly heavy orchestration, brooding chords, and the vigorous choruses.

Musically speaking, Act IV is one continuous crescendo. The music accelerates in minute-to-minute thrusts. The interpretation must convey gaiety, frenzy, love, mockery, despair, and finally death. The notes are all there, and the lyrics match them word for word. Each syllable counts. Each nuance reveals if the tenor can or cannot bring out the needed colouring and shading.

Then, there is Carmen, herself. There are very few passages in opera in which you are so completely dependent on your partner. The final scene in Carmen is one of these. After years of working together, Agnes Baltsa knows exactly how to shatter my reserve. She drives me to greater fury than any other partner I have worked with.

As I said before, there is a similarity, a bond, between Carreras the singer and Don José the protagonist. I do not refer to the José of the Merimée novel. He is a brutal man who judges impulsively and without hesitation. But I can identify with Don José of the opera.

First of all, I am a Spaniard too, with many facets to my personality. Then, like the José of the first act, I am a little shy, but at the same time, I am also very proud. When Carmen first explodes onto the stage, one hundred men surround her, vying for her attention. Yet one man, José, refuses to look at her. He has decided he will not be like the others. He will stand aloof and alone. I like that strategy. I might also act this same way if I wanted to win the attention of such a woman. Naturally, Carmen reacts to José's inattention almost immediately.

In love, however, José is a mere novice. He speaks affectionately to Micaela, but his feelings towards her are obviously that of brother and friend, not lover. It is only when José meets Carmen that his passion erupts. Yet his instincts warn him that his love for Carmen will be his damnation.

I cannot determine at exactly what point I, Carreras, stop identifying with Don José. I know I too am capable of similar, if not the same, desires and actions. I can be a man of impulse who is overwhelmed by enthusiasm, who loves suddenly and rapturously and later suffers excruciating jealousy. I can put myself easily into Don José's character because I understand the entire process of self-destruction. Words can hardly describe the effect Carmen has on him, it is so excessive. By the time they meet in front of the arena, José's love has turned to hate. Yet he will not renounce her. The tragic reality is obvious. He is no longer in control of himself. He is at the mercy of his most primitive instincts.

I don't think that any court in today's world would convict José of first-degree murder. Carmen drives him to madness. Only militant feminists could possibly side with Carmen.

The conflicts of the gypsy and the soldier are eternal. They not only fascinate the audience, they lure us, the actors. Carmen and Don José are forever.

As for Bizet's musical language, what terms can I use to describe it? His music defies explanation.

Carmen IS simply *Carmen.*

27

1988: Back in My World

Let's RETURN to 1988, the year of my own personal physical, spiritual, and artistic Renaissance. The life-threatening crisis, so disheartening since it seemed to signal the end of everything, was over. The first phase of my recovery lasted through spring. And in early summer, Carreras the singer began tracing slowly, carefully, his steps toward the ecstatic July comeback under Barcelona's Arch of Triumph.

Now it was time for the next episode, and I was preparing to fulfil my most heartfelt wish: to sing at last in an opera house, even if not yet precisely in an opera. This indoor recital was finally going to happen on September 16 in Vienna, the city, next to Barcelona, closest to my heart. I must stop here and give a few more details about this very special concert since it heralded for me the long, anxiously awaited return to my world of music.

I had already had a slight contact with the opera scene on two earlier occasions. The first was unique. At the beginning of July, Commencini's film *La Bohème* was presented in Barcelona as part of a motion picture festival. I was invited to the screening.

It was supposed to have been my film, but my illness

had posed a serious problem for the film company, and they had had to quickly find a suitable replacement for me. They had shot only a few minutes of me as Rodolfo; fortunately, the score had been prerecorded. Not just anyone can interpret an opera role to a pre-existing soundtrack, but my young Italian colleague Luca Canonici offered to do the part, and he played it most convincingly.

On the evening of this screen premiere, I was prey to conflicting emotions. To begin with it was a rare and peculiar sensation to hear my own voice coming out of the mouth of an alien Rodolfo. As much as I liked Luca, I naturally mourned for the lost opportunity of being able to portray "my" part myself. But I was happy to just be there at the screening.

My second contact with the opera world took place on August 8th in the Arena of Verona, Italy, where a truly magnificent concert was held to benefit my Foundation Against Leukemia. Many of my colleagues had participated, generously making a free gift of their talents. Because it was a marathon evening that could be fatiguing, I'd planned to do just the presentations, with no intention of singing. But when the programme neared its end, I could no longer resist the temptation, and I finally announced my return to the audience of Verona by singing "Granada."

A week later I was giving my second solo recital in Peralada, a town near Gerona, north of Barcelona. The music festival held there owes its existence to the initiative of my friend Carlos Caballé and has a distinctively charming atmosphere. Among its many events, an opera is staged outdoors, next to a fairy-tale castle which borders a small lake. People love to come here because the place is ideally located, close to Barcelona, yet near the beaches of Costa Brava. To crown a seaside vacation with an evening of music is a very appealing prospect, especially if the event is so extraordinary as the one held on the day of my recital. To everyone's surprised delight, Montserrat Caballé gave a so-called "street concert" in the early evening.

It began when a piano was placed in the heart of the village. Suddenly, a unique mood seemed to prevail, a celebration uniting villagers and tourists, noisy babies, happy children, and barking dogs. The surrounding streets were jammed with onlookers who sat on rooftops, climbed out of the windows, and crowded tiny balconies to hear Spain's most famous diva. The guests of honour were Queen Sofia and her sister Princess Irene, the former Queen Annemarie of Greece, and Diana, the Princess of Wales.

Only a short hour later, these ladies moved from the village square to the gardens of the castle, where they gave me the honour of their presence at my recital. The evening turned out to be glorious yet intimate, even though it was televised live throughout the world.

Now I was due for a few days of relaxation. I would need energy to concentrate fully on a most important date, a song recital in the Vienna Staatsoper. Its Director, Claus Helmut Drese, had already made the arrangements in June, long before he even knew if I'd ever walk onto a stage again. But Drese believed in my future and so did I. He suggested that we call my concert simply An Evening with José Carreras. Our conversation took place when I was still completely enraptured by the spectacle of Michael Jackson performing for a sold-out audience of cheering thousands in a football stadium. Seeing this brilliant extravaganza infected me with the performer's bug; I was suddenly overwhelmed by a hunger for the stage, for the public, for success. I couldn't help but agree wholeheartedly with all of Drese's wonderful suggestions.

I clearly understood the pivotal significance of a concert in Vienna. It would be my hour of truth in front of a

public that could compare me to many of my past performances under this same roof. Up to now, after my illness, I
had sung only in two open air recitals where the necessities
of space required the use of a microphone. The first was
under Barcelona's Arch of Triumph, the second in a small
summer locality. Now the circumstances would be completely different. I would be singing indoors, on the stage
of one of the most famous opera houses in the world.

My preparations were intense. Because it was Vienna, I
was spurred by the ambition not to make things easy for myself, so I changed the expected programme by adding three
songs that I'd never before sung in public. These three son-
nets, written by Francesco Petrarca and set to music by
Franz Liszt, were to be my tribute to the Austrian city of
music and its widely practised and cherished art of song.

Vienna is a city truly in love with artists! Opera and theatre occupy a privileged position, uniting public interest in
a way that's unheard of anywhere else in the world. I suspect that it's probably the only city where the director of
the opera, no matter his name, appears as a regular news
item on the front pages of the daily papers. These historic
names have included Richard Strauss, Karl Bohm, Herbert
von Karajan, Lorin Maazel, and now Claus Helmut Drese.
In the long and colourful history of the Staatsoper, several
directors have had to resign prematurely because of various pressures whereas some others have acknowledged defeat by themselves. The so-called "opera scandal," usually
of concern only to insiders, is a tradition inseparable from
Vienna. Fans relish the gossip and spread it through the
streets and corners of the city.

People who've never set foot inside an opera house
suddenly become impassioned about the Staatsoper. The
most trivial incidents concerning that venerable house
become the talk of the town and front page news. For ex-

ample, there's still city wide laughter about an unusual show stopper that occurred during a performance of *Tosca* in December 1982. The third act firing squad failed to materialize because the uniformed supers were having a cozy get-together in a nearby bar instead of parading across the roof of Castel Sant'Angelo. No deadly barrage to kill off Cavaradossi. My hapless colleague Nicola Martinucci fled into the wings, leaving his Tosca, a baffled Montserrat Caballé, alone on the stage. There was a storm of laughter instead of a storm of bullets. During the tragic finale, Montserrat bravely carried on, lamenting her invisible lover, and leaving her public to accept this hopeless task.

Other more serious events have originated in and around the Vienna Opera. When, for example, an irate Herbert von Karajan announced his resignation in 1964 from the Viennese stage, even the Austrian Parliament joined the operatic fray and debated the "Karajan Case" for several full days. At night pro-Karajan slogans were smeared on the windows and walls of the Staatsoper. During these "days of outrage," there was hardly a performance without some sort of disturbance. The simple fact is that when the Viennese public takes an artist into their hearts, the intensity of their feelings is beyond words. Usually this affection takes the form of a life-long commitment. I had ample proof of this commitment during that memorable time in September.

In the days preceding the concert, my fans mounted a banner with the inscription *Wilkommen, José* across the facade of the opera house. This was an achievement in itself, as in Vienna a government permit is needed for absolutely everything. It goes without saying that this sign made me very happy, as did the rediscovery of my friends in the "José Carreras Fan Club." When their spokesperson greeted me with a few phrases in Catalan, obviously having learned them just for the occasion, I sensed how joyous they all felt about my return.

The concert organizers, however, had a few problems. They received more than 20,000 ticket requests for a house with the capacity of 2200! What to do? The management decided to enlarge the seating by covering over the orchestra pit for more seats and placing chairs on the stage. It was my privilege to set a new house record. In the history of the Staatsoper, never have so many people crowded in to attend an artistic event. Many fans waited through the night to obtain the scarce tickets.

There was yet another gesture of welcome. A few days before the concert I was invited to the Austrian Ministry of Culture, where I was made an Honorary Member of the Vienna Staatsoper. With this title in my heart on the evening of September 16 I walked out onto the stage, accompanied by my pianist Vincenzo Scalera. The stage was decorated with red and yellow flowers that matched the national colours of Spain and Austria, and a Catalan flag was draped over the Presidential box. Among important politicians in the audience, I was privileged to have the Chancellor of the Republic and the Mayor of Vienna. But what gave me the greatest joy was to see among the spectators the doctors who had treated me during long months in Barcelona and in Seattle. I had invited them especially, and Drs. Thomas and Buckner had flown in from Seattle, while Professor Rozman and Drs. Grañena and Permanyer had travelled from Barcelona.

It is an incomparably electrifying experience to return after a long and forced absence to the stage where you have garnered great successes in more than a hundred past appearances. When I first walked on stage, the audience greeted me with such affection and thunderous enthusiasm that the very atmosphere became charged with an undefinable yet concrete "something," that rarest of theatrical moments. I felt the surge of something special, something extraordinary. The audience felt it too. This reciprocity was translated into an evening that shall remain unparalleled.

In terms of sheer emotion, my first seconds on the Viennese stage were almost harder to control than during my appearance at the Arch of Triumph in Barcelona. I suppose that the intimacy of an opera house helps to increase this tension, for in a closed space everything is intensified, and sound reverberates with enormous strength. A scream rose up from the seated audience; a long ovation followed from the thousands who stood up to greet me. This was the beginning of a concert which would reach the epic proportions of a short Wagnerian opera, something I didn't suspect at the time. Indeed, it lasted over three hours, inconceivable for a mere song recital.

It was being transmitted live by Austrian television, which on that evening proved that everything is possible in Vienna. Viewers who waited at home for newscasts or sports results had to exercise unusual patience for over an hour because the concert transmission ended at 11:15 instead of the usual 10 pm. The cameras simply stayed on during the added pieces and encores. When the news broadcasts finally began, they were repeatedly interrupted by live shots of the applauding audience in the house or of the thousands of people outside in the opera square who followed the concert from its beginning on a giant video screen, despite the cold drizzle.

The audience inside was transfixed. I could judge the spectators' passion not by sound alone. Somehow the effervescent mood in the house expanded and enveloped the stage. Then there were all the people seated just behind the grand piano. I found myself in an arena surrounded by a multitude who didn't want to let go of me. It was fantastic, exhausting. After all, when the official part of the programme ended I had already sung more than twenty songs. But I knew what I owed to the public. Who could resist their joy? I sang encore after encore. "Thank you, José, thank you!" The people were shouting to me from all over the house. Flowers rained on the stage; the aisles became dangerously crowded. A banner was unfurled in the middle of the orchestra. My Viennese fans had painted their own version of the title of Edvard Grieg's "I love thee," and it became "We love you." I thanked the audience by singing this song which had been my very first number in Barcelona and which now became my fifth encore and the twenty-fifth song of the evening.

I felt completely drained. And yet I just had to thank personally all those people who had spent hours craning their necks at the giant video screen out in the cold night. However, I wasn't able to reach the small podium built in the middle of the opera square for this purpose. I tried, but the pressure of the crowds against the stage door was too much. Though hefty employees of the opera were shielding me, we had to flee back into the house for fear that I might be crushed by the surging multitude.

Instead I was taken out onto the balcony of the director's office, where I could at least wave at the thousands of waiting people.

My personal guests, the physicians from Seattle and Barcelona, simply couldn't believe their eyes and ears. Naturally, they all knew what usually takes place in an opera house or in a concert hall, but they'd never in their lives witnessed a scene like this one in Vienna. Even the members of my own family, Maria Antonia, Alberto, and his wife Marisa, who'd shared many extraordinary opening nights with me over the years, were moved profoundly by the Vi-

As Columbus, a role composed for me by Leonardo Balada. Originally scheduled for Fall 1987, Balada's new modern opera, *Cristobal Colon,* was postponed until my return to the stage. I sang the title role of this world premiere in September 1989, in "my" house, the Liceo in Barcelona. The cast included Montserrat Caballé and Victoria Vergara. It was an artistic success, produced to celebrate the 500th anniversary of the discovery of America. We made operatic history.

May 1989: I kept my vow to sing my first American recital after remission as a benefit for the Fred Hutchinson Cancer Research Center in Seattle. Medical personnel and music lovers in the audience greeted me with unbelievable affection. As you can see, the feeling was mutual. My joy was beyond words.

Below :
overwhelmed at
being able to
return to opera in
Vienna. Curtain
call after *Carmen*,
January 1990.

A moment in Comencini's film of La Bohème—of which I was only able to shoot a few minutes. Marcello is played by Gino Quilico.

A very special meeting on October 8, 1988 with my colleagues Giuseppe di Stefano and Luca Canonici. Luca replaced me as Rodolfo in the film La Bohème when I became ill.

Medea (played by Montserrat Caballé) was my first opera, and Giasone, my first role debut, after two years of forced absence—festivals of Merida and Peralada, summer 1989. Left, a dramatic moment with Maria Gallego as Glauce. Below, responding to the enthusiastic audience.

This photograph was taken around the time of taping *West Side Story*.

I respect every form of music, as long as it's good music. Among my platinum and gold crossover records (*West Side Story, Misa Criolla,* and others) was *South Pacific.* Its gold

record was presented to me during my 40th birthday party, December 5, 1986. Six months later I had to leave the music industry. When I returned, I finished an interrupted recording assignment of *La Juive* and went on to other records. Proceeds from many of my tapings help the leukemia foundation.

Proof that it is possible to overcome the near impossible: a year after my bone marrow transplant I was playing—and winning—a charity football match for my leukemia foundation. Salzburg, 1989.

A cheque from the José Carreras International Leukemia Foundation for a hospital in Vienna. Since 1988 benefit concerts and donations yielded over eight million dollars for research and treatment in more than nine countries. Fund raising is a major part of my life today.

Josep as Don José, Vienna 1985. There is a bond between us. I, too, am shy, proud, impulsive, capable of overwhelming enthusiasm and self-destruction. In a relatively short time, I sang this part more than a hundred times. *Carmen* signalled my international operatic comeback: I sang it in Japan and Austria, right after *Medea* and *Colon*, which were produced at home, in Spain.

Opposite: two different productions in the 80's with Agnes Baltsa as Carmen. Above, in London. Below, in Barcelona, Act II: I force Carmen to listen to me. We have had great success as a team in this opera.

With Helga Muller-Molinari as Carmen, Salzburg, 1986. Karajan directed me to end the Flower Song with pianissimo, which was extraordinary—and very successful.

A very contented man . . . at the intermission during *Carmen* in the Arena of Verona.

In blind rage, I stab Carmen (Agnes Baltsa), Vienna, 1990.

As Don José in Act III at the Met, 1987: his process of self-destruction has begun.

Below, the end: I realize that I killed Carmen, Vienna, 1990.

A role debut in 1990: as the Hebrew warrior in *Samson et Dalila,* summer festival of Peralada. As it often happens in the life of an opera singer, I recorded this work earlier (February 1989) and it was not released until the year after my performing it for the first time on stage.

July 7, 1990—under the stars on the immense stage of the Baths of Caracalla, Rome. They said it couldn't be done: to get three very busy tenors, with world-wide schedules, to sing together. And would it be a competition, rather than a concert? Not at all. My two friends, Placido Domingo and Luciano Pavarotti, and I had an unforgettable time performing together, with our favourite charities reaping the benefit. It was an historic event, full of atmosphere, fun, energy, and wonderful singing.

The fact that our concert happened before the World Cup soccer championship added to the excitement. Our orchestra was 198 members strong and we were conducted by the fiery Zubin Mehta. Over 100,000 spectators sought the 6000 seats. A billion and a half television viewers saw us through satellite linkups.

Top, during a medley of songs, Luciano's turn. Bottom, the last note of the concert and of "Vinceró," from "Nessun dorma" *(Turandot)*, our unison victory cry! The media dubbed us the trio of the century—in the concert of the century.

Relaxing, once again, in San Francisco after many years of absence. Having given a benefit recital in New York's Carnegie Hall I came to the West Coast to film a private concert of Misa Criolla in San Francisco's venerable Basilica. The footage became part of a semidocumentary film with the central character a Spanish singer, not unlike myself. June 1990.

ennese overflow of affection.

I felt immensely happy, so much so that I didn't mind it at all when the next morning I couldn't follow my normal sleepyhead routine. I couldn't sleep late because I was startled out of my bed by the sharp ringing of the telephone. The caller was Herbert von Karajan. He had watched the concert on television and wished to congratulate me.

With the concert behind us, we decided to explore culinary Vienna. I took my guests from Spain and the United States to the famous wine suburb, Grinzing, where we dined in a restaurant famed for gigantic Viennese *schnitzel*, so large that they hang over the rim of the plates. To round off our celebrating, I also introduced them to a legendary confectioner's shop in the centre of the city. After all, Vienna is not only known to be a musical metropolis, but also the pastry capital of the world.

That so very lucky concert in Vienna represented a huge slap on the back for the new life I was beginning. In fact, I finally could say to myself, "You're here again! Welcome back!" All this is evidence that music not only makes people feel good, bringing them peace, joy, and happiness, but also has the power to heal. Examples of medical practices involving music abound in different eras and cultures, from the Indian healer who would frighten illness away by chanting wild songs, to the present day psychiatrist who uses music therapy by very specific prescription.

As I sang I applied a double measure of this therapy to myself. Just as praise is an expression of supportiveness that everyone needs, my first post-illness successes had far-reaching significance in providing me with the necessary incentive to continue toward ultimate restoration. Deep down it's actually a simple process that will develop in everyone under similar circumstances, but I do consider it to be one of the more fascinating developmental functions of

our nature. Whatever the case may be, I was feeling better
from day to day.

In the weeks that followed, I managed to include in my
schedule some guest appearances on television. I also took
part in a benefit concert in Paris and sang recitals in Co-
logne and Barcelona, as well as in Munich.

At the end of November, I recorded a Christmas programme for a popular television show in Madrid called
"Saturday Night." I sang several pieces with Montserrat
Caballé, a duet of "Silent night" in four different languages. That same day I had a meeting with our Prime Minister, Felipe Gonzales, who once more assured me of his
desire to collaborate with my Foundation Against Leukemia and to help me establish a solid financial base for it.
During our conversation I was able to inform the Prime
Minister that the proceeds of my comeback recital on July
21 in Barcelona had enabled the Hospital Clinico to reno-
vate its Hematology walk-in section so that it now could
boast some extremely modern treatment rooms.

At the beginning of December, I went to Paris where I
accepted a rather large contribution to the Foundation in a
most unorthodox manner. I presided over the inauguration festivities of a high fashion house. Afterwards *tout
Paris* gathered in the famous Le Doyen restaurant for the
gala banquet. Understandably, it was very gratifying when
the well-known French radio station EUROPE dedicated a
whole day to broadcasting a former interview with me on
the morning news which included a review of the mile-
stones in my career and a playing of many of my recordings.
I was thus constantly with the listeners until the small hours
of the night.

On December 5th I went home to celebrate a special
day with my family. It was my forty-second birthday and I

couldn't help looking back. Yet the past year seemed so far away to me, so distant. I had the feeling that I had been caught in a nightmare and then finally been freed by a good angel. Now we could laugh about certain incidents that had happened in Seattle. We retold old stories, and in the end someone in our group quoted the Spanish proverb that seemed to fit my situation: "Fate carries some on its wings, and others it drags behind." After dragging me for a time, fate chose to carry me on its wings. And for this I am thankful to God.

Four days later I was standing in the Sala Nervi in the Vatican, about to give a very special concert to which I had been looking forward for many weeks. Six thousand people were in the great auditorium, and director Franco Zeffirelli was acting as Master of Ceremonies. On that December 9th, I sang the solo part of the *Missa Criolla* and *Navidad nuestra* by Ariel Ramirez for the first time in public. I had recorded these compositions in the summer of 1987, just a few days before the outbreak of my leukemia. The day after the concert, Pope John Paul II granted a private audience to my wife, my children, and me. For all of us, but particularly for Alberto and Julia, it was an unforgettable experience.

Another comeback took place just before Christmas. I set foot in a recording studio for the first time since my illness. It was in Budapest, and the result was my third *Tosca*, in which I was partnered by Eva Marton, with Juan Pons as my antagonist and Tilson Thomas as the conductor. My previous *Toscas* had been with Montserrat Caballé and Ingvar Wixell under Colin Davis the first time, with Katia Ricciarelli and Ruggero Raimondi under Herbert von Karajan the second.

On Christmas eve we again performed the *Missa Criolla*, this time in Oviedo. I have to admit that I had special reasons for singing this beautiful Argentinian Mass precisely on this day and in this place. Sentiment played a part, and I was also motivated by thankfulness. It was the anniversary of my temporary release for the 1987 holidays from the Hutchinson Clinic in Seattle.

But this was a different time now and a different place. After the New Year, January 7, 1989, I sang in an Opera Gala in the National Auditorium in Madrid together with Montserrat Caballé, Victoria de los Angeles, Alfredo Kraus, Juan Pons, Ana Maria Gonzalez, and Isabel Rey. Our Royal Family was present. We were celebrating the inauguration of the Spanish presidency of the European Community and the Fifth Centennial of the Discovery of America. Later in the month I gave a concert at La Scala, Milan. Other commitments followed on the heels of this event. In February I sang at the annual Vienna Opera Ball—under the baton of Placido Domingo! Also in February Agnes Baltsa and I collaborated in the recording of *Samson et Dalila* in Munich.

And so my calendar began to fill up with dates. The everyday life of an artist took hold of me again although in a slightly different, newer version.

28

Reflections and Conclusions

WHEN I REFLECT on all that has happened to me in the last few months, I am struck by one meaningful fact: I have experienced and learned more in this relatively brief time than I did in all the years of my life put together. Today I live my life with a much deeper awareness than ever before.

My perception of the concept of love has widened. I've discovered that to be appreciated and loved by people as a whole is a wonderfully life-giving feeling. When all is said and done, love is the one absolutely essential ingredient in our lives. We are creatures who constantly hunger for it. And there are many different kinds of love we need to feel. For our children—tender, warm affection. For our relatives—a sense of commitment and kinship. For friends—fondness and respect. Between two people who form a couple, a personally unique blend of intimacy, romance, and attachment. I believe in the fundamental premise that human beings need to give and receive love to reach an emotional equilibrium and stability. And I am fully convinced that love comes only to those who give it.

It was infinitely helpful during my illness to be shielded by so much general affection. Today I continue receiving expressions of devotion that are much more concentrated than in the past years. I don't believe that such intense devotion flows so generously my way because I'm a well-known opera singer. No, I feel that it's directed to me because I am someone who wouldn't give up without a fight, someone who has seemingly become for many people a symbol of struggle against illness and adversity. People find in my fate guidance to overcome their sufferings, sufferings which may be much worse than mine have ever been. What more could I wish for than that my case serve as a precedent of survival and of hope for others?

If you are ready and willing to learn, life can teach you something new every day. As the years pass, these lessons will bring you small, inevitable changes in the way you look at things, in your approach to life. But only an event of transcending force can shake you up enough to make you ask some fundamental questions and bring about a far-reaching, drastic change in you. This is something we all believe we know, but don't really understand. It's only when we are confronted with a shattering situation that we realize all its implications.

Such was my case. For months I had nothing but time on my hands, time to reflect on all aspects of my life. So many things crowded my mind, so many conclusions. For example, I realized how superficial and life-draining it was for someone to assert, "Oh, I'd love to do this, but I'm afraid I don't have the time!" This kind of statement is nothing more than a vulgar lie. Can you conceive of anything more enriching than to accomplish what you've always wanted? And who's to say you don't have the time?

All my life, up to a certain day, I've thought myself to be a happy man. Was it true? Maybe I was, but perhaps I wasn't.

It doesn't matter now, because I am persuaded that it's not necessary for me to have my old, pre-illness lifestyle in order to be happy. Even if it's true that I need to keep active, to keep busy, I am also sure that after so many years of going full steam ahead, it will do me a world of good to lighten up on the throttle and simply slow down. In fact, I have a real need to do so. I remember confessing earlier to a fundamental change in my outlook concerning some things, happenings, and encounters, that used to have very little value for me. Now things that I completely ignored have become astonishingly important to me.

But the opposite has also happened. Other factors in my life have lost the meaning and value I attributed to them at one time.

Singing is the only constant that has survived all the changes in my life. I have no doubt that it will always remain my most important and cherished activity. Yet even in this I feel differently. There's a subtle distinction, perhaps limited to difference of degree, which is due to two things. I don't need to kill myself working any more and I don't have to prove anything to anyone, absolutely nothing at all. And most importantly, there's nothing more I have to prove to myself, for I am aware of what I can do and I know where I stand. What more do I want?

Only this, above all else, that singing be my reason to rejoice, not to advance my career. This is a special boon I promised myself. I will sing because I need to sing. I will sing for me. And if, at the same time, my joy becomes a pleasure for those who listen, then I will have given my artistic life the full meaning it should have.

Left. Seattle, May 1989.

Appendix A

FIRST PERFORMANCES OF JOSÉ CARRERAS
IN HIS ROLES

Norma (Flavio)	1970		Barcelona
Nabucco	1970		Barcelona
Lucrezia Borgia	1970		Barcelona
Maria Stuarda	1971		London
I Lombardi	1971	concert	Paris
Lucia di Lammermoor	1971		Menorca
La Traviata	1971		Prague
Rigoletto	1971		Teneriffe
Faust (Siebel)	1971		Barcelona
Maruxa	1971		Madrid
La Bohème	1972		Parma
Luisa Miller	1972		Barcelona
Don Carlos	1972		Toulouse
Madame Butterfly	1972		New York City O.
El Giravolt	1972		Barcelona
Mefistofele	1972		London
Catarina Cornaro	1972		London
I Lombardi	1972	concert	Carnegie Hall, NY
Ballo in Maschera	1972		Parma
Adriana Lecouvreur	1972		Barcelona
La Pietra di Paragone	1972	concert	Alice Tully Hall, NY
L'Elisir d'Amore	1973		Marseille
Tosca	1873		New York City O.
Beatrice di Tenda	1973		Turin

Il Giuramento .... 1974................................. Berlin
Messa da Requiem (Verdi) 1974................................. Turin

Jerusalem................................ 1975........ concert .... Turin

Don Carlos (5-Act Version) 1977................................. Milan
Robeto Deveroux .... 1977................................. Aix-en-Provence

Der Rosenkavalier (Tenor) 1978................................. Hamburg
Werther .... 1978................................. San Francisco
La Forza del Destino........... 1978................................. Milan

Aida.. 1979................................. Salzburg
Andrea Chenier.................... 1979................................. Barcelona
La Gioconda .... 1979................................. Geneva

La Juive .... 1981........ concert .... Vienna

Carmen .... 1982................................. Madrid

Romeo et Juliette .... 1983................................. Barcelona
Turandot .... 1983................................. Vienna·
Il Trovatore........................... 1983................................. London
Herodiade .... 1983................................. Barcelona

Simone Boccanegra .... 1984................................. Vienna

I Pagliacci .... 1986................................. Madrid
Poliuto .... 1986........ concert .... Vienna

Medea .... 1989................................. Merida
Cristobal Colon .... 1989................................. Barcelona

Samson et Dalila .... 1990................................. Peralada

Appendix B

DISCOGRAPHY

1972

La Pietra del Paragone (Rossini)
Wolff, Bonazzi, Elgar; Reardon, Foldi, Diaz
The Clarion Concerts Orchestra and Chorus, Jenkins
Vanguard

1973

Un Giorno di Regno (Verdi)
Cossotto, Norman; Wixell, Sardinero, Ganzarolli
Ambrosian Singers, Royal Philharmonic Orchestra,
 Gardelli
Philips

1974

Canco d'Amor i de Guerra (Martinez Valls, Capdevilai Victor)
Caballé, Decamp; Sardinero, Gonzalez
Orfeo Gracienc, Barcelona Symphony Orchestra,
 Ros Marba
Columbia (Sp.)

1975

Thais (Massenet)
Moffo, Bacquier; Diaz
The Ambrosian Opera Chorus, New Philharmonia
  Orchestra, Rudel
RCA

Elisabetta, Regina d'Inghilterra (Rossini)
Caballé, Masterson, Creffield; Benelli, Jenkins
Ambrosian Singers, London Symphony Orchestra,
  Masini
Philips

Il Corsaro (Verdi)
Norman, Caballé; Mastromei, Grant
Ambrosian Singers, New Philharmonia Orchestra,
  Gardelli
Philips

1976

José Carreras Sings
I Lombardi: La mia letizia infondere (Verdi)
La Forza del Destino: La vita e inferno - Oh, tu che in seno
  agli angeli (Verdi)
Luisa Miller: Oh! fede negar potessi - Quando le sere al
  placido (Verdi)
Un Ballo in Maschera: Forse la soglia attinse - Mas se m'e
  forza perderti (Verdi)
Jerusalem: L'infamie - O mes amis, mes freres
  (Verdi)

Il Giuramento: La Dea de tutti i cor - Bella adorata incognita,
   Compiuta e omai - Fu celeste (Mercadante)
Il Duca d'Alba: Inosservato - Angelo casto e bel (Donizetti)
Maria di Rohan: Nel fragor della festa - Alma soave e cara
   (Donizetti)
Adelson e Salvini: Ecco, signor, la sposa (Bellini)
Il Figliuol Prodigo: Il padre! - Tenda natal (Ponchielli)
Royal Philharmonic Orchestra, Benzi
Philips

I Due Foscari (Verdi)
Ricciarelli; Cappuccilli, Ramey
Chorus and Symphony Orchestra ORF, Gardelli
Philips

Der Rosenkavalier (Strauss)
Lear, Von Stade, Welting; Bastin
Rotterdam Philharmonic Orchestra, de Waart
Philips

Tosca (Puccini)
Caballé; Wixell, Ramey
Chorus and Orchestra of the Royal Opera House, Covent
   Garden, Davis
Philips

Macbeth (Verdi)
Cossotto; Milnes, Raimondi
Ambrosian Opera Chorus, New Philharmonia Orchestra
   of London, Muti
EMI

Lucia de Lammermoor (Donizetti)
Caballé; Ahnsjo, Sardinero, Ramey, Bello
Ambrosian Opera Chorus and New Philharmonia
   Orchestra, Lopez Cobos
Philips

José Carreras Sings Opera Arias
Il Corsaro: Come liberi volano i venti . . . Tutto parea
   sorridere;
   Eccomi prigionero (Verdi)
Ambrosian Singers, New Philharmonia Orchestra,
   Gardelli
I Due Foscari: Notte, perpetua notte . . . Non maledirmi
Symphony Orchestra ORF, Gardelli
Tosca: E lucevan le stelle (Puccini)
Royal Opera House, Covent Garden, Davis
Elisabetta, Regina d'Inghilterra:
Della cieca fortuna . . . Sposa amata (Rossini)
London Symphony Orchestra, Masini
Lucia de Lammermoor: Tombe degl'avi miei . . . Fra poco
   a me ricovero (Donizetti)
Samuel Ramey, Ambrosian Singers, New Philharmonia
   Orchestra, Lopez Cobos
Philips

1977

Simon Boccanegra (Verdi)
Freni; Cappuccilli, Ghiaurov, van Dam
Chorus and Orchestra of Teatro alla Scala, Abbado
DG

Turandot (Puccini)
Caballé, Freni; Plishka
Chorus of l'Opera du Rhin, Philharmonic Orchestra,
  Strasbourg, Lombard
EMI

José Carreras Canta Zarzuela
Por el humo, *Dona Francisquita* (Vives)
Noche de amor, noche misteriosa, *El ultimo romantico,*
  (Soutullo, Vert)
Cancion hungara, *Alma de Dios* (Serrano,)
Cancion guajira, *La alegria del batallon* (Serrano)
Cuantas veces solo, *Los de Aragon* (Serrano)
Raquel, *El huesped del Sevillano* (Guerrero)
Jota, *La Bruja* (Chapi)
De este apacible rincon de Madrid,
  Luisa Fernanda (Morena Torroba)
Paxarin, tu que vuelas, *La picara molinera* (Luna)
Romanza, *El caserio,* (Guridi)
English Chamber Orchestra, Ros Marba
Philips, Zambra

1978

La Vida Breve (Falla)
Berganza, Nafe; Pons
London Symphony Orchestra, Garcia Navarro
DG

La Battaglia de Legnano (Verdi)
Ricciarelli; Manuguerra, Ghiuselev
Chorus and Symphony Orchestra ORF, Gardelli
Philips

Un Ballo in Maschera (Verdi)
Caballé, Payne; Wixell, Ghazarian
Chorus and Orchestra of Royal Opera House
  Covent Garden, Davis
Philips

José Carreras Sings
Granada (Lara)
Malia (Tosti)
Parlami d'amore, Mariu (Bixio)
Non ti scordar di me; Ti voglio tanto bene (de Curtis)
Core 'ngrato (Cardillo)
Be my love (Brodszky)
Lolita (Buzzi-Peccia)
Musica proibita (Gastaldon)
Das Land des Lachelns -Dein ist mein ganzes Herz
  (Lehar)
English Chamber Orchestra, Benzi
Philips

Don Carlos (Verdi)
Freni, Baltsa, Gruberova; Ghiaurov, Cappuccilli,
  Raimondi, van Dam
Chorus of the Deutsche Opera, Berlin Philharmonic,
  Karajan
EMI

Otello (Rossini)
Von Stade; Pastine
Ambrosian Opera Chorus, Philharmonia Orchestra,
  Lopez Cobos
Philips

1979

La Bohème (Puccini)
Ricciarelli, Putnam; Wixell, Hagegard, Lloyd
Chorus and Orchestra of the Royal Opera House,
  Covent Garden, Davis
Philips

José Carreras Sings
Manon Lescaut: Donna non vidi mai (Puccini)
Turandot: Nessun dorma (Puccini)
Zaza: O mio piccolo tavolo (Leoncavallo)
I Pagliacci: Recitar! - Vesti la giubba (Leoncavallo)
La Boheme: Testa adorata (Leoncavallo)
I Zingari: Principe! Radu io son - Dammi un amore
  (Leoncavallo)
Andrea Chenier: Un di all'azzurro spazio (Giordano)
La Gioconda: Cielo e mar (Ponchielli)
L'Amico Fritz: Ed anche Beppe amo! (Mascagni)
Tosca: Intenditi con Dio (Gomes)
L'Arlesiana: E la solita storia (Cilea)
London Symphony Orchestra, Lopez Cobos
Philips

Aida (Verdi)
Freni, Ricciarelli, Baltsa; Cappuccilli, van Dam,
  Raimondi
Vienna Opera Chorus, Vienna Philharmonic, Karajan
EMI

Stiffelio (Verdi)
Sass; Manuguerra, Ganzarolli
Chorus and Orchestra ORF, Gardelli
Philips

Cavalleria Rusticana (Mascagni)
Caballé, Hamari, Varnay; Manuguerra
I Pagliacci (Leoncavallo)
Scotto; Nurmela, Benelli, Allen
Southend Boys' Choir, Ambrosian Opera Chorus,
  Philharmonia Orchestra, Muti
EMI

Tosca (Puccini)
Ricciarelli; Raimondi
Chorus of the Deutsche Opera Berlin, Berlin
  Philharmonic, Karajan
DG

José Carreras Sings Tosti
La serenata; Segreto; Marechiare; Vorrei morire;
  Malia; Chanson de l'adieu; L'ultima canzone; L'alba
  separa della luce; l'ombra; Aprile; Ideale; Sogno; A
  Vucchella; Non t'amo piu; Good-bye
English Chamber Orchestra, Muller
Philips

Katia Ricciarelli and José Carreras Sing Love Duets

With Linda Finnie

Madama Butterfly: Bimba, bimba non piangere
   (Puccini)

I Lombardi: Dove sola m'inoltro? . . . Per dirupi e per
   foreste (Verdi)

Poliuto: Questo pianto favelli . . . Ah! fuggi da morte
   (Donizetti)

Roberto Devereux: Tutto e silenzio (Donizetti)

Ambrosian Opera Chorus, London Symphony
   Orchestra, Gardelli
Philips

1980

Werther (Massenet)
Von Stade, Buchanan; Allen
Orchestra of the Royal Opera House, Covent Garden,
   Davis
Philips

Il Trovatore (Verdi)
Ricciarelli, Toczyska; Masurok
Chorus and Orchestra of the Royal Opera House,
   Covent Garden, Davis
Philips

José Carreras Sings Neapolitan Songs
O sole mio; Santa Lucia luntana; Funiculi funicula;
   Torna a Surriento; Core 'ngrato, and others
English Chamber Orchestra, Muller
Philips

Tristia, Op. 18
Lelio, Op 14b (Berlioz)
With Thomas Allen
John Alldis Choir, London Symphony Orchestra,
  Davis
Philips

Canciones Romanticas
Valencia; Amapola; Morucha; Ay, ay, ay; La partida;
  Princesita; El Guitarrico; Jurame; Estrellita;
  Maitechu mia
English Chamber Orchestra, Stapleton
Philips

Spanish Songs
(Nin, Halffter, de Falla, Toldrá, Abril,
  Turina) Zanetti, piano
Ensayo

José Carreras Sings
I Vespri Siciliani: Recitativo & aria: E di Monforte il
  cenno - Giorno de pianto (Verdi)
Rigoletto: Scena & romanza: Ella mi fu rapita - Parmi
  veder le lagrime (Verdi)
Ernani: Recitativo & cavatina: Merce, diletti amici -
  Come rugiada al cespite (Verdi)
Attila: Scena & romanza: Qui del convegno e il loco -
  Che non avrebbe il misero (Verdi)
L'Elisir d'Amore: Una furtiva lagrima (Donizetti)
Roberto Devereux: E ancor la tremenda porta non si dis-
  chiude - A te diro (Donzetti)
Stabat Mater: Cujus animam gementem (Rossini)

Guglielmo Tell: Non mi lasciare, o speme - O muto asil
   del pianto (Rossini)
London Philharmonic Orchestra, Lopez Cobos
Philips

1981

La Périchole (Offenbach)
Berganza; Bacquier, Senechal
Chorus and Orchestra of the Capitole de Toulouse,
   Plasson
EMI

L'Enfant Prodigue (Debussy)
Norman; Fischer-Dieskau
La Damoiselle Élue
Cotrubas
Women's Choir of South German Radio, Stuttgart
   Radio Symphony Orchestra, Bertini
Orfeo

1982

Carmen (Bizet)
Baltsa, Ricciarelli; van Dam
Chorus of the Opera de Paris, Berlin Philharmonic,
   Karajan
DG

1983

Messa di Gloria (Puccini)
Ambrosian Singers, Philharmonia Orchestra,
  Scimone
Erato

Ave Maria
Halleluja, *Messias* (Handel); Panis angelicus (Franck);
  Pieta, Signore (Stradella); Pregaria (Alvarez); Heilig,
  heilig, heilig *Deutsche Messe,* (Schubert); Ave Maria,
  Repentir (Gounod); Agnus Dei (Bizet); Quattro pezzi
  sacri: Laudi alla vergine Maria (Verdi); Jesus bleibet
  meine Freude, *Kantate* (Bach)
Vienna Choirboys, Vienna Symphony, Harrer
Philips

José Carreras Sings Schubert:
Aus Vier Canzonen, D 688
  Nr. 3: Da quel sembiante appresi
  Nr. 4: Mio ben ricordati
  Nr. 1: Non t'accostar all'urna
Weyrauch: Adieu!
Wagner: Attente, Mignonne; Les deux grenadiers
Liszt: Drei Sonnette von Francesco Petrarca: Pace non
  trovo; Benedetto sia il giorno; Il 'vidi in terra angelici
  costumi
Schneider, piano
Acanta

Petite Messe Solennelle (Rossini)
Ricciarelli, Zimmermann; Ramey
Ambrosian Singers, Sheppard and Berkowitz,piano,
  Scimone Philips

Lou Salome (Sinopoli)
With Lucia Popp
Stuttgart Radio Symphony Orchestra,Sinopoli
Polygram

You Belong to My Heart
English Chamber Orchestra, Garcia Asensio
Philips

The Sound of Christmas—Christmas with World Stars
José Carreras: White Christmas
CBS

Turrandot (Puccini)
Marton, Ricciarelli; Bogart
Chorus and Orchestra of the Vienna State Opera,
  Maazel
CBS

Love Is . . .
Because you're mine, As time goes by, The way we were,
  and others
Robert Farnon and his Orchestra
Philips

1984

Messa da Requiem (Verdi)
Tomowa-Sintow, Baltsa; van Dam
Chorus of the National Opera of Sofia Vienna State Opera Chorus, Vienna Philharmonic, Karajan
DG

French Opera Arias
Faust: Quel trouble inconnu me penetre . . . Salut! Demeure chaste et pure (Gounod)
Romeo et Juliette: L'amour, l'amour
(Gounod)
Polyeucte: Source delicieuse (Gounod)
Le Cid: Ah! Tout est bien fini! . . . O Souverain, o Juge, o Pere (Massenet)
Sappho: Ce monde que je vois . . . Ah! qu'il est loin, mon pays! (Gounod)
Herodiade: Ne pouvant reprimer . . . Adieu donc, vains objets (Massenet)
La Juive: Rachel! quand du seigneur (Halevy)
L'Africaine: Pays merveilleux . . . O paradis (Meyerbeer)
Le Roi d'Ys: Puisqu'on ne peut flechir . . . Vainement, ma bien aimee (Lalo)
Carmen: La fleur que tu m'avais jetee (Bizet)
Orchestra of the Royal Opera House, Covent Garden, Delacote
EMI

Spanish Songs
by Falla, Mompou, Ginastera, Guastavino, Obradors,
  Turina
Katz, piano
Philips

L'Elisir d'Amore (Donizetti)
Ricciarelli; Nucci, Trimarchi
Chorus and Orchestra RAI Turin, Scimone
Philips

Mi Otro Perfil
Ten Spanish and Catalan songs
José Carreras with Orchestra
Zafiro

West Side Story (Bernstein)
Te Kanawa, Troyanos; Ollmann
Bernstein
DG

                            1985

Merry Christmas
Silent night; Oh holy night; Lullaby; Ave Verum; Ave
  Maria; Joy ot the world; El cant tels ocells; Mary's Boy
  Child; Adeste fideles; Mille cherubini; White Christ-
  mas; Jingle bello; It's Christmas time this year, Nav-
  idad
Vienna State Opera Choir Osterreicher
CBS

Mes que mai
José Carreras Sings two Catalan Songs with Nuria Feliu
PDI, Barcelona

Fedora (Giordano)
Marton, Kincses; Martin
Hungarian Radio and Television Symphony Orchestra
  and Chorus, Patane
CBS

La Forza del Destino (Verdi)
Plowright, Baltsa; Bruson, Burchuladze, Pons
Ambrosian Opera Chorus, Philharmonia Orchestra,
  Sinopoli
DG

Romanza Final
Arias from the film about Spanish tenor Julian Gayarre
Zafiro

                        1986

South Pacific (Rodgers)
Te Kanawa, Vaughan; Patinkin
London Symphony Orchestra, Tunick
CBS

Poliuto (Donizetti)
Ricciarelli; Pons
Chorus of the Vienna Singing Academy, Vienna
  Symphony, Caetani
CBS

Andréa Chenier (Giordano)
Marton; Zancanaro
Hungarian State Orchestra, Chorus of the Hungarian
  State Radio and Television, Members of the
  Children's Choir of the Hungarian State Opera, Patané
CBS

1987

Madama Butterfly (Puccini)
Freni, Berganza; Pons
Ambrosian Opera Chorus, Philharmonia Orchestra,
  Sinopoli
DG

La Bohème (Puccini)
(Soundtrack from the Comencini film) Hendriks,
  Blasi; Quilico
National Orchestra of France, Radio of France Chorus,
  Conlon
ERATO

Manon Lescaut (Puccini)
Te Kanawa; Coni, Tajo
Chorus and Orchestra of the Teatro
  Comunale de Bologna, Chailly
DECCA

Et portaré una rosa
José Carreras Sings ten Catalan songs
Zafiro

Misa Criolla (Ramirez)
Navidad en verano, Navidad nuestra
Salve de Laredo Chorale, Bilboa Society Chorale,
  Ocejo and Sanchez
Philips

1988

José Carreras, The Comeback Concerts
(Released in 1989)
Barcelona, Arc de Triomfe, 21.7.1988
Ich liebe dich (Grieg); José Carreras welcomes the
  audience; Malia (Tosti); Canticel (Toldra); El cant dels ocells
  (Mompou); Jo et pressentia com la mar (pop. Cat. song); No
  puede ser (Sorozabal); L'emigrant (Vives); Nessun
  dorma (Puccini)
Peralada, Jardi del Castell, 13.8.1988
L'heure exquise (Hahn)
Le manoir de Rosemonde (Duparc)
Damunt de tu, nomes les flors (Mompou)
Nunca olvida (Turina)
Del cabello mas sutil (Obradors) and others
Wien, Staatsoper, 16.9.1988
Granada
Scalera, Schneider, piano
Pilz Acanta

José Carreras Presenta La Grande Notte a Verona,
  August 8, 1988
Leo Nucci: Largo al factotum
Ghena Dimitrova: Suicidio
Peter Dvorsky: Donna non vidi mai
Sonia Ghazarian: Mi chiamano Mimi

Giacomo Aragall: L'anima ho stanca
Ruggero Raimondi: Ella giammai m'amo
Elena Obraztsova: Voi lo sapete
Ferruccio Furlanetto: La calunnia
Natalia Troitskaya: Ritorna vincitor
Luca Canonici: E la solita storia
Montserrat Caballé: Pleurez mes yeux
Placido Domingo: Canto a la espada
Samuel Ramey: Mentre gonfiarsi l'anima parea dinanzi
   a Roma
Aprile Millo: Pace, pace, mio Dio
Vincenzo La Scola: Una furtiva lagrima
Mara Zampieri: Casta Diva
René Kollo: In fernem Land
Silvano Carroli: Credo in un Dio crudel
Eva Marton: Sola, perduta, abbandonata
Juan Pons: Di provenza il mar
Antonio Ordonez: Sento avvampar nell'anima
Ileana Cotrubas: Azael, Azael! Pourquoi m'as-tu quittée?
José Carreras: Granada
Polyphon

**José Carreras Live from the Vienna State Opera
(September 16, 1988)**
Apres un Reve (Fauré)
Ouvre tes yeux bleus (Massenet)
Los dos miedos (Turina)
Tengo nostalgia de ti (Nacho)
Intima (Nacho)
I vidi in terra angelici costumi (Liszt)
Benedetto sia'l giorno
Pace non trovo (Liszt)
Sole e amore (Puccini)
Terra e mare

Menti all'avviso
Apri (Tosti)
Non t'amo piu
A vucchella
L'ultima canzone
Core 'ngrato (Cardillo)
Dicitencello vuie (Falvo)
Scalera, piano
Polyphon/Polygram

Recital at Gran Teatre del Liceu, Barcelona, November 8, 1988
Ecco la tomba . . . Deh 'tu bell 'anima (Bellini)
Vaga luna, che inargenti
Gia il sole del Gange (Scarlatti)
Per la gloria d'adorarvi (Bononcini)
Oh come il fosco . . . Quell 'alme pupille (Rossini) and
  others
Schneider, piano
Polyphon

Tosca (Puccini)
(Released in 1990)
Marton; Pons, Gati
Hungarian State Radio and Television Chorus,
  Hungarian State Orchestra, Tilson Thomas
SONY Classical

1989

La Juive (Halevy)
(recorded in 1986 and 1989)
Varady, Anderson; Gonzales, Furlanetto
Ambrosian Chorus, Philharmonia Orchestra, Ambrosian Opera Chorus, Almeida
Philips

José Carreras sings Andrew Lloyd Webber
Memory; The phantom of the opera (with Barbara Dickson); The music of the night; Wishing you were somehow here again; All I ask of you (with Barbara Dickson); Pie Jesu; Tell me on a Sunday; Half a moment; There's me; Starlight express; Unexpected song; Love changes everything
Accompaniments scored and conducted by George Martin
WEA Records

Caballé, Carreras Live in Moscow, September 5, 1989
Intima (Nacho); Pieta Signore (Stradella); Sposa, son disprezzata (Vivaldi); O Patria . . . De tanti palpiti (Rossini); Chanson de L'adieu (Tosti); Elegia eternan (Granados); La Maja y el ruisenor; Core 'ngrato (Cardillo); El vito (Obradors); L'emigrant (Vives)
Zanetti, piano
Polyphon

Samson et Dalila (Saint-Saens)
(Released in 1991)
Baltsa ; Estes, Burchuladze
Bayreuth Rundfunk Orchestra, Davis
Philips

1990

Italian Opera Composers' Songs
Rossini: L'esule
Donizetti: L'amor funesto; le crepuscule; Una
    lacrima, Amor marinaro; Il sospiro
Bellini: La ricordanza; Malinconia, ninfa gentile; Vaga
    luna che inargenti; Per pietá, bell'idol mio; Il fervido
    desiderio; Dolente immagine de Fille mia
Verdi: In solitaria stanza; Il poveretto; Il tramonto;
    Brindisi; L'esule
Katz, piano
SONY Classical

Pedro y el Lobo (Peter and the Wolf) (Prokofiev)
Sinfonia clasica
Obertura sobre temas hebreos
Marcha en si bemol mayor, op. 99
The Chamber Orchestra of Europe, Abbado
DG

Appendix C

VIDEOGRAPHY

1982

La Bohème (Puccini)
Stratas, Scotto; Morris
   Metropolitan Opera Orchestra, Levine
Paramount

1983

Turandot (Puccini)
Marton, Ricciarelli; Bogart
The Vienna State Opera Orchestra and Chorus,
   The Vienna Boys Choir, Maazel
MGM/UA Home Video

1984

The Making of West Side Story
(Released in 1989)
Te Kanawa, Troyanos: Ollmann
Bernstein
DG

I Lombardi (Verdi)
Dimitrova; Carroli, Bini
Chorus and Orchestra of La Scala, Milan, Gavazzeni
NVC/Thorn EMI/HBO

Verdi Requiem
Norman, M. Price; Raimondi
Edinburgh Festival Chorus and London Symphony
  Orchestra, Abbado
Thorn EMI/HBO

**José Carreras por José Carreras. Perfil de
  un Hombre. (Jose´ Carreras by José
  Carreras. Profile of a Man.)**
  (Released in 1990)
With Herbert von Karajan, Rudolf
  Nureyev, and others.
Classic Media/Selecta Vision (Sp)

1985

Andréa Chenier (Giordano)
Marton, Mazzieri; Cappuccilli, Frederici
Chorus and Orchestra of La Scala, Milan, Chailly
NVC/Home Vision

Messa da Requiem (Verdi)
  (Released after 1990)
Tomowa-Sintow, Baltsa; van Dam
Wiener Staatsopernchor, Chor der Nationaloper
  Sofia, Wiener Philharmoniker, Karajan
SONY Classical

Silent Night with José Carreras
White Christmas; O come all ye faithful; Jingle bells;
  Silent night and others
Kultur

The Final Romance
Based on the life of Julian Gayarre
Sydne Rome, Antonio Ferrandis, and Montserrat Caballé
Produced and directed by José M. Forque
Kultur

1986

South Pacific (Rodgers and Hammerstein)
The London Sessions
Te Kanawa, Vaughan; Patinkin
London Symphony Orchestra, Tunick
CBS/Fox

Don Carlos, (Verdi)
(Released after 1990)
Izzo d'Amico, Baltsa; Furnaletto, Cappuccilli
Berliner Philharmoniker, Wiener Staatsopernchor,
  Salzburger Konzertchor, Karajan
SONY Classical

1987

José Carreras in Concert, January 9, 1987
Malia; Non amo piu; L'ultima canzone (Tosti);
  Fenestra che lucive (Bellini); O begli occhi (Denza);

Nebbi (Respighi); Mattinata (Leoncavallo);
Cancion al arbol del olvido (Ginastera); La rosa y el sauce
(Guastavino); Fado (Halffte); No puede ser (Sorozabal);
Sole e amore, Avanti Urania, Menti all 'avviso
(Puccini); Core 'ngrato (Cardillo); Il Lamento de
Federico (Cilea); Granada (Lara); Tonight (Bernstein);
Dicitencillo a'sta campagna vosta (Falvo);
Nessun dorma (Puccini)
Scalera, Piano
Kultur

Carmen
Baltsa, Mitchell; Ramey
The Metropolitan Opera Chorus and Orchestra, Levine
DG Video

1988

**Jose' Carreras Presenta La Grande Notte a Verona,
  August 8, 1988**
(Released in 1989)
Leo Nucci: Largo al factotum
Ghena Dimitrova: Suicidio
Peter Dvorsky: Donna non vidi mai
Sonia Ghazarian: Mi chiamano Mimi
Giacomo Aragall: L'anima ho stanca
Ruggero Raimondi: Ella giammai m'amo
Elena Obraztsova: Voi lo sapete
Ferruccio Furlanetto: La calunnia
Natalia Troitskaya: Ritorna vincitor

Luca Canonici: E la solita storia
Montserrat Caballé: Pleurez mes yeux
Placido Domingo: Canto a la espada
Samuel Ramey: Mentre gonfiarsi l'anima parea dinanzi
  a Roma
Aprile Millo: Pace, pace, mio Dio
Vincenzo La Scola: Una furtiva lagrima
Mara Zampieri: Casta Diva
René Kollo: In fernem Land
Silvano Carroli: Credo in un Dio crudel
Eva Marton: Sola, perduta, abbandonata
Juan Pons: Di provenza il mar
Antonio Ordonez: Sento avvampar nell'anima
Ileana Cotrubas: Azael, Azael! Pourquoi m'as-tu quittée?
José Carreras: Granada
Polyphon/Polygram

Misa Criolla (Ramirez)
Mission Dolores, San Francisco, June 1990
(Released in 1991)
Coro de la Basilica del Socorro, Cuarteto Andino,
  A. Ramirez, piano; Segade
Philips Classics

1990

Carreras, Domingo, Pavarotti in Concert, July 7, 1990
Carreras: I lamento di Federico; Core 'ngrato;
  Granada; L'improvviso

Domingo: O paradis; Dein ist mein ganzes Herz; No
  puede ser; E lucevan le stelle
Pavarotti: Recondita armonia; Rondine al nido; Torna
  a Suriento; Nessun dorma
Carreras, Domingo, Pavarotti: Finale medley—Maria;
  Tonight; 'O paese d'o sole; Cielito lindo; Memory;
  Ochi tchorniye; Caminito; La vie en rose; Mattinata;
  Wien, Wien, nur du allein; Amapola; O sole mio
Encores: O sole mio, Nessun dorma
Orchestra del Maggio Musical Fiorentino
Orchestra del Teatro dell'Opera de Roma,Mehta
DECCA/LONDON

Credits and Photographers

© ACTION PRESS: Section I: Plate 2 (top right)

© CLIVE BARDA: Section III: Plate 9 (top)

ANTONI BOFILL: Section II: Plate 11 (bottom), Plate 12 (top),
   Plate 13 (top); Section III: Plate 5 (all), Plate 9 (bottom), Plate 13
   Plate 13

© CHRISTINA BURTON: Section I: Plate 12 (bottom)

CARLOS CABALLÉ/A. BOFILL: Section III: Plate 4 (bottom)
CARLOS CABALLÉ/MONTACCHINI: Section I: Plate 8 (bottom)

ROBERT CAHEN: p. 8, p. 232; Section II: Plate 7, Plate 9 (bottom);
   Section III: Plates 2 and 3 (top), Plate 11, Plates 14 and 15
   (all), Plate 16
■ **ROBERT CAHEN. 19 PARK ROAD, BURLINGAME, CA 94010.**
   Telephone: (415) 342-6333. Fax: (415) 342-8009. *"SPECIALIST*
   IN PERFORMING ARTS AND PORTRAITURE."

JIM CALDWELL: p. 100

JOSÉ CARRERAS/S.A.F.R., RAVENNA: pp. 154-5

CBS/SCHOELLER: Section III: Plate 6 (top)

DEUTSCHE GRAMMOPHON/LAUTERWASSER: Section II,
   Plate 4 (top)

271

ZOE DOMINIC: Section I: Plate 13 (bottom); Section II: Plate 14

EUROPEAN AMERICAN PRODUCTIONS: Section I;
  Plate 10 (bottom)

EUROPEAN AMERICAN PRODUCTIONS/NORBERT
  KÖSSLER: Section I: Plate 10 (top)

© FABIAN-SYGMA-ERATO: Section III: Plate 4 (top)

FOTO LAUTERWASSER: p. 122; Section II: Plate 11 (top)

FOTO FAYER WIEN: Frontispiece; Section I: Plate 15;
  Section III: Plate 3 (bottom), Plate 8, Plate 12 (bottom)
■ **FOTO FAYER WIEN, DAS PORTRAITSTUDIO.
  OPERNRING 6, 1010 VIENNA, AUSTRIA. Telephone:
  222/512 4811 or 222/512 8111. Fax: 222/513 7833.**
  *"SPECIALIST IN OPERA PORTRAITURE AND STAGE
  ACTION PHOTOGRAPHY."*

COURTESY OF FRED HUTCHINSON CANCER RESEARCH
  CENTER: pp. 56-7

HERBERT HUFNAGL: Section I: Plate 11 (bottom)

INTERVIU: Section II: Plate 15 (top)

CAROLYN MASON JONES for SAN FRANCISCO OPERA:
  p. 44, p. 114; Section II: Plate 6

WINNIE KLOTZ: p. 40, p. 166; Section I:
  Plate 16 (right); Section II: Plate 4 (bottom), Plate 8, **Plate 10;**
  Section III: Plate 12 (top)

NORBERT KÖSSLER, PRESS PHOTOGRAPHER: p. 64;
  Section II: Plate 5 (top); Section III: Plate 7 (bottom)

KURIER/PETER SCHAFFLER: Section I: Plate 3 (bottom)

© LECTURAS/LEUIS BOU: Section I: Plate 2 (top left)

© LELLI & MASOTTI: **Section II: Plate 5** (middle), p. 194

© ROBERTO MASOTTI: Section II: **Plates 2 and 3**

L'OSSERVATORE ROMANO, CITTÁ DEL VATICANO, SERVICIO

FOTOGRAFICO/ARTURO MARI: Section I: Plate 4

© PALFFY: Section I: Plate 16 (bottom)

© EL PERIODICO DE CATALUÑA: Section I: Plate 1

GREG PETERSON for SAN FRANCISCO OPERA: p. 78;
Section II: Plate 9 (top)

CARLOS PICASSO, COURTESY OF MARIO DRADI: pp. 206-7

PHOTO SCHAFFLER/SALZBURG: Section III: Plate 10 (top)
■ **PHOTO SCHAFFLER. SCHALLMOOSER HAUPTSTRASSE
29, A-5020 SALZBURG, AUSTRIA. Telephone: 0 662/74 367.
Fax: 662/8 79 1 76. *"SPECIALTY: OPERA GREATS IN
SALZBURG."***

PICCAGLIANI/TEATRO ALLA SCALA/MILAN: Section II:
Plate 1

© FRANÇOIS ROUSSILLON: Section III: Plate 1
■ **FRANÇOIS ROUSSILLON ET ASSOCIÉS. 61 AVENUE
DE LA MOTTE PICQUET, 75015 PARIS, FRANCE.
Telephone: 48 28 16 00. *"SPECIALISTS IN OPERA AND
BALLET PHOTOGRAPHY."***

S.A.F.R., RAVENNA: Section II: Plate 13 (bottom)

SCRIPT/AXEL ZEININGER: Section I: Plate 14 (bottom)

DONALD SOUTHERN: Section I: Plate 13 (top)

TV3 - TELEVISIÓ DE CATALUNYA/THE FINAL ROMANCE
(FILM): p. 182; Section II: Plate 15 (bottom)

UCLA, DEPARTMENT OF SPECIAL COLLECTIONS,
UNIVERSITY RESEARCH LIBRARY: Section I: Plate 12 (top)

UNESCO/INEZ FORBER: Section I: Plate 2 (bottom)

UDO SCHREIBER/US PRESS/VIENNA: Section III: Plate 6
(bottom), Plate 7 (top)

AXEL ZEININGER: Section I: Plate 3 (top); Section II: Plate 12
(bottom); Section III: Plate 16

All other photographs are from private collections.

Index

PRODUCTION ACKNOWLEDGEMENTS

Y.C.P. Publications, Inc. is grateful to the following individuals for their cooperation and help during the preparation of this book: Dr. Oddeliese Fuchs, discography research; Kathleen Herbert, editorial assistance; Rhonda Casper, colour analyst; Hildegarde Boos, Fiona Nagle, production assistance; members of The José Carreras Society of America.

Typesetter: Allan Stark, Goleta, CA

TELEPHONE ORDERS

For VISA/MASTERCARD only call TOLL FREE 1 (800) 247-6553 (800 hundred number only for orders please.) Ohio residents add appropriate sales tax. Have VISA or MASTERCARD ready. Please add $1.00 surcharge for credit card orders. Otherwise prices and SPECIAL OFFER are the same as for mail order. SINGING FROM THE SOUL cannot be sent to the British Commonwealth. However, Canadian orders are accepted.

Order Form

POSTAL ORDERS: Y.C.P Publications, Inc,
P.O. Box 931766, Los Angeles, CA 90093

Please send me _____ copy(ies) of SINGING FROM THE SOUL.

My Name_____
Print block letters
Address _____

_____

City/State/Zip
I am enclosing my cheque or Postal money order, payable to
Y.C.P. Publications, Inc.

❏   U.S. $27.95 plus_____ shipping/packing for one book.

❏   U.S. $ _____ plus_____ shipping/packing for the first book

and _____ for each additional book. Total books: _____.

SPECIAL OFFER

Get a 10% discount when you order 4 or more books. Meaningful and affordable gifts for every occasion and the holidays.

Please add SALES TAX for books shipped to California addresses.

SHIPPING

SURFACE MAIL:
U.S.A. - $2.50 for the first book, and 75 cents for each additional book.
CANADA and elsewhere outside U.S.A. (but not in the British
Commonwealth) US $4.00 for the first book, and US $1.50 for
each additional book. Allow 1 -12 weeks, depending on destination.
AIRMAIL:
EUROPE (but not the British Commonwealth) US $13.25 for the first book,
$10.00 for each additional book. ASIA - US $17.75 for the first book, and
US $14.00 for each additional book.

ATTENTION OVERSEAS READERS
This coupon is not valid in the British Commonwealth, but it is valid in
Canada and the rest of the world. Payments must be made in US dollars,
by Postal m.o. or by cheque drawn on a U.S. bank.
Availability and prices subject to change without notice.

◆◆◆

THIS BOOK IS AVAILABLE AT VOLUME DISCOUNTS FOR PROMOtIONAL
PURPOSES AND COMMUNITY PROJECTS. *Please write for information.*

WATCH FOR THE SIGN OF THE PHOENIX

NEC IGNI
CEDIT
NEC
FERRO

COMING SOON FROM Y.C.P. PUBLICATIONS

Books to read, and books to give

VISIONS FROM OPERA
Burning, unique visions of music and glimpses of lives that gave us those
visions. Words and color illustrations combined to convey a deeper
understanding of libretti - and of the men who created them.
There is nothing comparable in the world of opera books. See
the music - hear the pictures. Let the poetry of great opera touch you.

BALLET MAGICK.
(Previously SPRITES AND PRINCES, revised and expanded.) Unique
descriptions of most well loved ballets. Movement and story beautifully
illustrated in color. A must for beginners and aficionados of all ages.

COMING

MORE BALLET MAGICK.
(Previously ENCHANTERS AND PRINCESSES, revised and expanded.)
Enthralling sequel to BALLET MAGICK. Descriptions that make you
visualize. Color illustrations.

QUEEN MAB'S TALES.
Revised and expanded. Stories from Shakespeare with new color
illustrations. A collector's item. A charming introduction to great
literature.

THE RETURN OF QUEEN MAB.
More stories from Shakespeare. Color illustrations.

INTRODUCING CHILDREN TO OPERA

THE SECRET OF THE DOO DAH HOUSE
Caught in a summer storm 12-year-old Andrew, 10-year-old Laura, and
little Micki stumble upon a mysterious world of music where they meet
Mr.   Puccini, Mr. Mozart, Mr. Humperdinck, the Queen of the Night,
and many other fascinating characters....
A fun way to encourage youngsters to listen to grand opera. Imaginatively
illustrated in color.